The Grand Old Party: The History of

By Charles River Editors

John C. Fremont, the first Republican presidential candidate

About Charles River Editors

Charles River Editors provides superior editing and original writing services across the digital publishing industry, with the expertise to create digital content for publishers across a vast range of subject matter. In addition to providing original digital content for third party publishers, we also republish civilization's greatest literary works, bringing them to new generations of readers via ebooks.

Sign up here to receive updates about free books as we publish them, and visit Our Kindle Author Page to browse today's free promotions and our most recently published Kindle titles.

Introduction

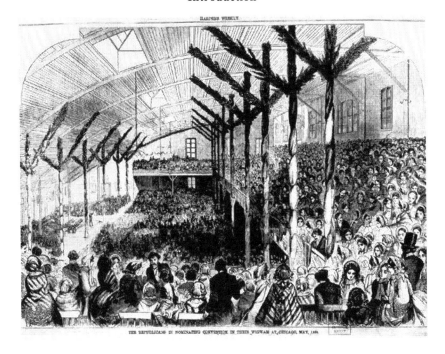

A cartoon depicting the 1860 Republican convention

The Republican Party

2016 has been one of the most unusual election years, and nothing represents the unprecedented nature more than the race for the Republican Party's presidential nomination, which featured over 15 candidates. As with most years, several candidates with various political experience, from former and current governors to Congressmen and Senators, ran, but the race also featured a number of political novices, one of whom is poised to be the party's nominee.

In a sense, all of that is fitting given the winding nature of the Republican Party's history. Now dominant in the American South, the party was anathema in the South for more than a century. Likewise, if someone asked a man on the street in the early 1900s to describe the Republican Party, he might point to Teddy Roosevelt's efforts on behalf of progressive politics and conservation, whereas a few years later, the Party was known as a protector of big business, and later law and order. During the Reagan Era, the words "small government" came to characterize the party, even as its leaders took one hit after another for wanting to limit social spending. Republicans were in office at the start of the Depression and the end of the Vietnam War.

Ultimately, the direction that the Republican Party has taken at any given time has been determined, for the most part, by the party leadership, which has traditionally made its voice most heard at the Republican National Convention, which convenes once every 4 years to nominate candidates for the presidency and vice-presidency. During its more than 150 years of existence, it has nominated saints and scoundrels, seen some men make it to the White House and others not. Its first successful candidate was assassinated, as was one of his successors a few decades later. It has survived through war and economic downturns, as well as the just as dangerous prosperity that seems to have been created by someone else. It remains one-half of the two party system that has almost always dominated American politics, even as many question its future. Of course, given the party's history, those who wonder how it will survive and move forward should probably take a look at what the party has already endured.

The Grand Old Party: The History of the Republican Party examines the formation of the GOP and the twists and turns the party has taken during its history. Along with pictures of important people, places, and events, you will learn about the GOP like never before.

The Grand Old Party: The History of the Republican Party

About Charles River Editors

Introduction

Chapter 1: Political Excitement

"The first Republican National Convention met in Philadelphia in June, 1856. The old Whig party had become disintegrated. Its National Convention, held in 1852, at which General Winfield Scott was nominated as a candidate for the Presidency, was destined to be its last. The Missouri Compromise had been repealed in 1854 and the Territories of Kansas and Nebraska had been opened to the introduction of slavery, which under the compromise had been prohibited. The Democratic party, ruled by the slave power of the South, was naturally pro-slavery and aggressive, while the Whig party, though having a large membership in the South, was in large part anti-slavery, but timid. Franklin Pierce, elected President in 1852, was the subservient tool of the slave power and ready to do its bidding. Political excitement at this time ran high throughout the country, and the matter of organizing a new party was agitated among the people and discussed in the public press." - John Tweedy, *A History of the Republican National Conventions from 1856 to 1908*

The Republican Party calls itself the Party of Lincoln, a reference to one of America's most famous men, but the seeds of the party extended back decades before Lincoln's presidency, even if it was not technically born until the eve of the Civil War.

When President Thomas Jefferson went ahead with the Louisiana Purchase, he wasn't entirely sure what was on the land he was buying, or whether the purchase was even constitutional. Ultimately, the Louisiana Purchase encompassed all or part of 15 current U.S. states and two Canadian provinces, including Arkansas, Missouri, Iowa, Oklahoma, Kansas, Nebraska, parts of Minnesota that were west of the Mississippi River, most of North Dakota, nearly all of South Dakota, northeastern New Mexico, northern Texas, the portions of Montana, Wyoming, and Colorado east of the Continental Divide, and Louisiana west of the Mississippi River, including the city of New Orleans. In addition, the Purchase contained small portions of land that would eventually become part of the Canadian provinces of Alberta and Saskatchewan. The purchase, which immediately doubled the size of the United States at the time, still comprises around 23% of current American territory. With so much new territory to carve into states, the balance of Congressional power became a hot topic in the decade after the purchase, especially when the people of Missouri sought to be admitted to the Union in 1819 with slavery being legal in the new state. While Congress was dealing with that, Alabama was admitted in December 1819, creating an equal number of free states and slave states. Thus, allowing Missouri to enter the Union as a slave state would disrupt the balance.

James Tallmadge of New York was the first to try to address this issue by limiting slavery in Missouri, and the Tallmadge Amendment sought to ensure that children of slave parents born in Missouri would automatically go free at the age of 25. The Senate ultimately got around this issue by establishing what became known as the Missouri Compromise. Legislation was passed that admitted Maine as a free state, thus balancing the number once Missouri joined as a slave state. Moreover, slavery would be excluded from the Missouri Territory north of the parallel

36°30′ north, which was the southern border of Missouri itself. As a slave state, Missouri would obviously serve as the lone exception to that line. The Missouri Compromise of 1820 staved off the crisis for the time being, but by setting a line that excluded slave states above the parallel, it would also become incredibly contentious.

Tallmadge

Despite the attempt to settle the question with the Missouri Compromise, the young nation kept pushing further westward, and with that more territory was acquired. After the Mexican-American War ended in 1848, the sectional crisis was brewing like never before, with California and the newly-acquired Mexican territory now ready to be organized into states. The country was once again left trying to figure out how to do it without offsetting the slave-free state balance was tearing the nation apart.

With the new territory acquired in the Mexican-American War, pro and anti-slavery groups were at an impasse. The Whig Party, including a freshman Congressman named Abraham Lincoln, supported the Wilmot Proviso, which would have banned slavery in all territory acquired from Mexico, but the slave states would have none of it. Even after Texas was annexed as a slave state, the enormous new territory would doubtless contain many other new states, and the North hoped to limit slavery as much as possible in the new territories.

The Compromise of 1850 was authored by the legendary Whig politician Henry Clay. In addition to admitting California to the Union as a free state to balance with Texas, it allowed Utah and New Mexico to decide the issue of slavery on the basis of what became known as "popular sovereignty", which meant the settlers could vote on whether their state should be a free state or slave state. Though a Whig proposed popular sovereignty in 1850, popular sovereignty as an idea would come to be championed by and associated with Democratic Illinois Senator Stephen Douglas. The Compromise also abolished the slave trade – though not the existence of slavery itself – in Washington, D.C. The Whigs commended the Compromise, thinking it was a moderate, pragmatic proposal that did not decidedly extend the existence of slavery and put slow and steady limits on it. Furthermore, it made the preservation of the Union the top priority.

The Little Giant, Stephen Douglas

Clay

However, even though it added a new free state, many in the North were upset that the Compromise also included a new Fugitive Slave Act, which gave slaveholders increased powers to recapture slaves who had fled to free states by providing that a slave found in a free state could be ordered captured by police or federal marshals and returned to the slaveholder without any trial or due process whatsoever. In addition, no process was provided for the accused escaped slave to prove that he was actually free. This outraged most Northerners, who saw it as an unconstitutional infringement on the rights of their states and the rights of the individual accused of being an escaped slave. It also raised the specter of southern slave owners extending grip over the law enforcement of Northern states.

By 1853 and 1854, Henry Clay's Compromise of 1850 came under withering assault, because the Compromise had not settled all territory needed to be admitted for statehood. In an attempt to organize the center of North America – Kansas and Nebraska – without offsetting the slave-free balance, Senator Stephen Douglas of Illinois proposed the Kansas-Nebraska Act.

Kansas-Nebraska proved to be the straw that broke the camel's back. First, the Kansas-Nebraska Act eliminated the Missouri Compromise line of 1820, which the Compromise of 1850 had maintained and had stipulated for over a generation that states north of the line would be free and states south of it *could* have slavery. This was essential to maintaining the balance of slave and free states in the Union. The Kansas-Nebraska Act, however, ignored the line completely and proposed that all new territories be organized by popular sovereignty. Settlers could vote whether they wanted their state to be slave or free.

When popular sovereignty became the standard in Kansas and Nebraska, the primary result was that thousands of zealous pro-slavery and anti-slavery advocates both moved to Kansas to influence the vote, creating a dangerous and ultimately deadly mix. Numerous attacks took place between the two sides, and many pro-slavery Missourians organized attacks on Kansas towns just across the border.

While men like John Brown acted militantly in the territories, politicians across the North, primarily Whigs and Free Soilers, were aghast over the Kansas-Nebraska Act. The suggestion that Congress could extend slavery into any unsettled territory violated some of their dearest held principles that slavery should not extend further. Whigs and Free Soilers in the North quickly coalesced against the "Slave Power", believing Southern influence in Washington had gone too far and now held the government in a strangle-hold. This coalescence first became known as the "anti-Nebraska" group, but it quickly vowed to form a new political party dedicated to keeping the Western territories free from slavery.

In his history on the early Republican National Conventions, John Tweedy explained how the new party began to coalesce: "A small club was organized in Washington, D. C, on June 19, 1855, at which a brief platform was adopted, in which it was stated that 'we do associate ourselves together under the name and title of The Republican Association of Washington, D. C.' On January 17, 1856, there was published and circulated largely by the Washington Association an appeal to the country to organize clubs. ... A call for a National Convention was issued January 17, 1856, for a meeting to be held at Pittsburg, Pa., on the 22d of February following."

Thus, a group of men met on February 22-23, 1856, a presidential election year, at Lafayette Hall in Pittsburgh, Pennsylvania. While many were among the event's organizers, there were some who had come after receiving the following summons:

"To the People of the United States:

"The people of the United States, without regard to past political differences or divisions, who are opposed to the repeal of the Missouri Compromise, to the policy of the present administration, to the extension of slavery into the territories, in favor of the admission of Kansas as a free state, and of restoring the action of the federal government to the principles of Washington and Jefferson, are invited by the national committee, appointed by the Pittsburg convention of February 22, 1856, to send from each state three delegates from every congressional district, and six delegates at large to meet in Philadelphia on June 17 next, for the purpose of recommending candidates to be supported for the offices of President and Vice-President of the United States."

The *New York Daily Times* reported on the first day of this convention, "Notes of preparation are sounding for the Republican National Convention, to meet tomorrow. The Republicans of the North are coming up grandly. Enthusiasm is abundant—confidence high, and unanimity remarkable. The East and the West are both strongly represented by men of right stamp, to give character and consistency to the proceedings of the Convention. It is not intended to nominate candidates—being an Informal Mass Convention, called by the Chairmen of the State Republican Committees to perfect the National organization and provide for a National Delegate Convention. Opinions are chiefly divided upon the character of the preliminary program. One section favors a call by the Central Committee at Washington. Another the apportionment of State delegates, and to set a time for the Convention. Caucuses are to be held this evening, to determine this and other delicate points. Very little is said of the candidates to be put forward. There is a general indisposition to precipitate events. The majority prefer waiting till early in the Summer before nominating. Cincinnati is much talked of as the place for holding the Convention. Two certainly, and perhaps three, addresses to the people, are in the pockets of delegates. One is in possession of the New-York delegation. It is long and able, and is understood to be a general review of the great national questions—taking strong Free-Soil but not Abolition ground. The other is understood to emanate from Ohio. It is explicit, and treats chiefly and strongly of Kansas matters and questions growing out of them. Neither address has seen the light, and both probably will be amended. A caucus will be held at the Mongolian House tonight, to discuss and amend them, if deemed advisable."

Among those listed as present at the convention were names both unknown and prominent, including "Edwin D. Morgan, Preston King, John A. King, Abijah Mann, Simeon Draper, George M. Grier, A. Oakey Hall, Joseph Keen, Geo. W. Blunt and Horace Greeley of New-York, Judge Hear, Davis and Dr. Stone of Massachusetts, Gov. Bingham of Michigan, Joshua B. Giddings of Ohio, and a large delegation —probably fifty—from the State, including Attorney-General Kimball, State Treasurer Gibeon, Judge Brinkerhoff and Ex-Judge Spalding." These men, ranging from governors to abolitionist newspaper editors, were almost all from the Northern states, which was no surprise given that the South was still dominated by the Democratic Party. There was, however, one exception: "Francis P. Blain is here as sole representative of the Southern chivalry, to keep the Convention in countenance. He is a delegate from the Republicans at Washington."

The convention, from its very inception, was a hodge-podge of groups gathering together for the common purpose. The author of the article explained, "The German Republicans of Ohio, at a very large meeting in Cincinnati, I think, appointed Charles Reemiin Delegate. He is here representing the Free German sentiment, and is gladly welcomed. The Ohio Germans are strongly Republican, and it is a pleasant indication for the Party in that State, their strength being great. Pennsylvania is making a good show of hands. Much is said to-day of the Know-Nothings at Philadelphia. Everybody looks to see a split, and it will not be strange if this influences action here somewhat. Still, it may not. The Committee of Reception is headed by Hon. Thomas M. How, and consists of sixteen prominent citizens of Pittsburgh, the Convention opens at Lafayette Hall, at 10 o'clock to-morrow. The Republican editors in attendance were invited to meet this afternoon in Convention, but delayed until the arrival of the Western trains at 10 o'clock to-night. They propose to unite on a plan of action. They are numerous, particularly from Ohio, which abounds in Republican sharp-shooters."

In the 19th century, as in the 21st, there was much concern and interest in how the convention would organize itself, and particularly in how the delegates from each state would be represented. Of course, the main difference is that the delegates were not chosen by the public: "A series of resolutions are handed about quietly to-night. They are short and pithy. They declare that having assembled in Mass Convention with a view to perfect an organization of the people against the extension of Savory, and In favor of administrative reform; it is proper to declare— First, the appointment of a National Committee to represent the Republican Party, to be formed of one delegate from each State; second, recommending the Republicans to assemble in National Convention at Cincinnati on the second Monday in June next —the Committee aforesaid to Issue a call; third, in each Convention each State to be entitled to three delegates from each Congressional district, to be appointed by District Conventions, and six delegates at large. No action will, of course, be had of these or any other till to-morrow. Up to this hour upwards of one hundred delegates have arrived, and others are expected by the night trains."

The delegates who gathered that weekend did a remarkable amount of work in a very small amount of time and by the time they left for their homes, they had issued their first platform:

> "This Convention of Delegates, assembled in pursuance of a call addressed to the people of the United States, without regard to past political differences or divisions, who are opposed to the repeal of the Missouri Compromise; to the policy of the present Administration; to the extension of Slavery into Free Territory; in favor of the admission of Kansas as a Free State; of restoring the action of the Federal Government to the principles of Washington and Jefferson; and for the purpose of presenting candidates for the offices of President and Vice-President, do

> "Resolved: That the maintenance of the principles promulgated in the Declaration of Independence, and embodied in the Federal Constitution are essential to the preservation of our Republican institutions, and that the Federal Constitution, the rights of the States, and the union of the States, must and shall be preserved."

Up to this point, the men were on pretty solid ground, sticking to general ideas that everyone could agree on. However, this changed with the next resolution, and the ones that followed:

"Resolved: That, with our Republican fathers, we hold it to be a self-evident truth, that all men are endowed with the inalienable right to life, liberty, and the pursuit of happiness, and that the primary object and ulterior design of our Federal Government were to secure these rights to all persons under its exclusive jurisdiction; that, as our Republican fathers, when they had abolished Slavery in all our National Territory, ordained that no person shall be deprived of life, liberty, or property, without due process of law, it becomes our duty to maintain this provision of the Constitution against all attempts to violate it for the purpose of establishing Slavery in the Territories of the United States by positive legislation, prohibiting its existence or extension therein. That we deny the authority of Congress, of a Territorial Legislation, of any individual, or association of individuals, to give legal existence to Slavery in any Territory of the United States, while the present Constitution shall be maintained.

"Resolved: That the Constitution confers upon Congress sovereign powers over the Territories of the United States for their government; and that in the exercise of this power, it is both the right and the imperative duty of Congress to prohibit in the Territories those twin relics of barbarism--Polygamy, and Slavery."

Finally, the convention had to deal with the nation's future concerning the Western states. It concluded:

"Resolved, That Kansas should be immediately admitted as a state of this Union, with her present Free Constitution, as at once the most effectual way of securing to her citizens the enjoyment of the rights and privileges to which they are entitled, and of ending the civil strife now raging in her territory.

"Resolved, That the highwayman's plea, that 'might makes right,' embodied in the Ostend Circular, was in every respect unworthy of American diplomacy, and would bring shame and dishonor upon any Government or people that gave it their sanction.

"Resolved, That a railroad to the Pacific Ocean by the most central and practicable route is imperatively demanded by the interests of the whole country, and that the Federal Government ought to render immediate and efficient aid in its construction, and as an auxiliary thereto, to the immediate construction of an emigrant road on the line of the railroad.

"Resolved, That appropriations by Congress for the improvement of rivers and harbors, of a national character, required for the accommodation and security of our existing commerce, are authorized by the Constitution, and justified by the obligation of the

Government to protect the lives and property of its citizens.

"Resolved, That we invite the affiliation and cooperation of the men of all parties, however differing from us in other respects, in support of the principles herein declared; and believing that the spirit of our institutions as well as the Constitution of our country, guarantees liberty of conscience and equality of rights among citizens, we oppose all legislation impairing their security."

Though he's best remembered today for his expeditions across the United States, John C. Fremont, the "Pathfinder," ended up being chosen as the Republican candidate that summer. He would go up against Democrat James Buchanan and fall short, but as Tweedy pointed out, the Republican Party would remain on the scene: "There was great enthusiasm for Fremont and Dayton throughout the North and West. Clubs were organized and mass meetings held in almost every town. The cry, 'Free speech, free press, free soil, free men, Fremont and victory,' was a popular one, and heard on every hand. Pennsylvania, the home of James Buchanan, the Democratic candidate for President, was the principal battleground through the summer and early fall, and the Republicans had high hopes of carrying the state in the October state election, but were to be sadly disappointed. The vote was, however, close and the result in doubt for several days. The Republicans were encouraged to believe that the Quakers had not voted in the state election, but would surely vote for President and for Fremont. Whether they did or not, the result in November was the same as in October and the electoral vote of Pennsylvania was given to Buchanan. ... The general result was a great blow to the young party that had been so hopeful of success. But it was not to be. An overruling Providence had decreed otherwise. The time had not yet come. There was to be a wait of four years for the election of Abraham Lincoln."

Chapter 2: The Party of Lincoln

Ironically, the first Republican President was one of the most fervent Whig holdouts in the mid-1850s. Although destined to be forever associated with the Republican Party, Lincoln wasn't yet convinced that the Party of Clay was on its last legs when the Republican Party first began to form. The one term Congressman ran as a Whig for Senate in 1854, and it was only after that loss that Lincoln began to gather among Republican circles.

Lincoln didn't just become a Republican: he became a remarkably influential one. At the Party's first national convention, the Illinois delegation nominated Lincoln for the Vice Presidency. He didn't win, but nonetheless received 110 votes before the convention decided on William Dayton of Ohio. Lincoln was pleased with himself. He denied suggestions that he was eying a Congressional seat, though everyone knew he still held hopes for a seat in the U.S. Senate.

Just two years later, amid yet another controversy – the Supreme Court's *Dred Scott* decision – the Illinois Republican Party nominated Abraham Lincoln for the U.S. Senate. In his acceptance speech, Lincoln warned the nation that "A house divided against itself cannot stand. I believe this government cannot endure permanently half slave, half free. I do not expect the union to be dissolved – I do not expect the house to fall – but I do expect it will cease to be divided. It will become all one thing, or all the other." In his now-famous "House Divided" speech, Lincoln set the stage for a campaign against a formidable opponent – the Little Giant himself.

Throughout the Fall of 1858, Lincoln and Stephen Douglas participated in seven three-hour debates throughout Illinois. This unprecedented method of campaigning drew national attention, one that is still often idealized even today among those who feel politics is too bitterly partisan.

The main theme of the debates was the topic being discussed across the nation: slavery and, specifically, its expansion into the unorganized territories. In substance, Lincoln argued stances very similar to those he uttered in his Peoria speech. He lamented the expansion of slavery but insisted that states where slavery already existed were entitled to maintain the institution there. Lincoln also argued forcefully against popular sovereignty, which he thought threatened to expand slavery across the entire nation.

Douglas's strategy was to label Lincoln a radical "Black Republican." Douglas' position on slavery was that, if it were reduced to an essentially local issue through popular sovereignty, it would no longer divide the nation as it had in recent decades. While he morally opposed slavery, he also pragmatically thought it could not thrive in the Western territory because the land there was inhospitable to slave labor anyway.

His most damning charge against Lincoln, however, was that the Republican candidate advocated the social and legal equality of the races. Douglas wanted to deny citizenship to all African-Americans, which the Supreme Court had ruled in the *Dred Scott* case. In his rebuttal, Lincoln offered one of his most quotable moments: "I protest against the counterfeit logic which concludes that, because I do not want a black woman for a slave, I must necessarily want her for a wife. I need not have her for either, I can just leave her alone."

Portrait of Dred Scott

The apex of the debate came when Lincoln brought up the issue of the *Dred Scott* decision. In his argument, Lincoln raised the contradiction between the decision and Douglas' concept of popular sovereignty. *Dred Scott* had decided that Congress could do nothing to limit slavery in a territory. Lincoln, then, thought popular sovereignty left voters with no decision: how could they effectively limit slavery in a territory if Congress didn't have the authority to do so? Douglas replied that local voters could defund methods of protecting slave property within a territory, which would essentially, though not legally, eliminate slavery.

Douglas' reply became known as the Freeport Doctrine, and it damaged his national popularity significantly. Southerners were hoping he would defend the nationalization of slavery, but he didn't. Northerners hoped for a more effective, legal, way of restricting slavery from a territory. Douglas was pinned somewhere in the middle. His chances of winning the Presidency in 1860 – a topic of much discussion in 1858 – were badly reduced.

Regardless, though, Douglas won the 1858 Senate election, making Lincoln a loser in a race yet again. But this time was different. Lincoln had gained national stature because of the Lincoln-Douglas debates, and now he was poised for something big.

Throughout 1859, Illinois papers began to mention Lincoln as a Republican candidate for President. Lincoln was humbled, though a bit dumbfounded. He thought himself more suited for the Senate, where he could orate and discuss ideas, and moreover there were Republicans of much greater national prominence on the East coast, particularly William Seward. Lacking any administrative experience, he wasn't sure he would enjoy being President. Regardless, it was a great honor, and he quietly thought the idea over.

William Seward

   Going into the Republican Convention in May of 1860, the Republicans were hopeful. The Democratic Party, partly because of Stephen Douglas, was deeply divided over slavery, and it had broken into a Northern and Southern faction. By dividing their votes, they were likely handing over the presidency to a Republican Party that would barely win a plurality across the nation. Sensing opportunity, the Republicans were careful in selecting their candidate. Many delegates considered the frontrunner, William H. Seward, to be too radical. With a divided electorate, there were fears that Seward's radicalism might lose the Midwest for the Republicans.

   At the Convention, Seward's support maintained steady throughout the rounds of voting. Lincoln polled a surprising second place on the first ballot. He gradually picked up votes from other Midwestern candidates until he was selected as the Republican Party's Presidential nominee on the third ballot. Hanibal Hamlin of Maine was nominated as the Vice Presidential nominee.

   Tweedy described the moment Lincoln officially earned enough delegates: "When quiet to some extent was restored, Mr. Cartter, the chairman of the Ohio delegation, arose and said: "I arise, Mr. Chairman, to announce the change of four (4) votes from Mr. Chase to Abraham Lincoln." "This announcement giving Lincoln a majority was greeted by the audience with the most enthusiastic and thundering applause. The entire crowd rose to their feet, applauding rapturously, the ladies waving their handkerchiefs, the men waving and throwing up their hats by thousands, cheering again and again. The applause was renewed and repeated for many minutes." When partial order had been restored, many gentlemen were striving to get the floor. Many states changed their votes to Lincoln, so that when the result of the ballot was announced Lincoln had 364 votes out of a total of 466, with 234 as necessary to a choice, and Abraham

Lincoln was declared by the president as the choice of the convention as its candidate for President of the United States. The cheering broke out anew, and amid the booming of cannon, was taken up by the thousands outside of the Wigwam who had been notified of the result of the balloting by men at the skylight of the roof above the delegates, who took bulletins to the front of the building."

Lincoln, in keeping with the traditions of the time, was not present when he was nominated to the presidency. However, the president of the convention, Edwin D. Morgan, spoke for the group, when he concluded, "Every symptom, every sign, every indication accompanying the Convention in all its stages, are a high assurance of success, and I will not doubt, and none of us doubt, that it will be a glorious success. Allow me to say of the nominees, that, although it may be of no consequence to the American people or to you, they are both personally known to me. It was my good fortune to have served with Mr. Lincoln in the Congress of the United States, and I rejoice in the opportunity to say that there was never elected to the House of Representatives a purer, truer, nor a more intelligent and loyal Representative than Abraham Lincoln. The contest through which he passed during the last two years has tried him as by fire; and in that contest in which we are about to go for him now, I am sure that there is not one man in this country that will be compelled to hang his head for anything in the life of Abraham Lincoln. You have a candidate worthy of the cause; you are pledged to his success; humanity is pledged to his success; the cause of free government is pledged to his success. The decree has gone forth that he shall succeed. ... Now, gentlemen, that we have completed so well, so thoroughly, the great work which the people sent us here to do, let us adjourn to our several constituencies; and thanks be to God who giveth the victory, we will triumph."

Lincoln had essentially been chosen for his moderate stance on slavery. Unlike many other viable Republican contenders, Lincoln was less likely to alienate valuable "battleground" states like Illinois, Indiana and Ohio. At the same time, the more staunchly abolitionist Northeast would have no better alternative.

Throughout the fall, the campaign broiled on. As was customary, Lincoln did no active campaigning. Presidential candidates in the mid-1800's did not campaign on their own behalf; surrogates did the work for them. His supporters portrayed Lincoln as a man of great integrity from humble origins. Opponents conjured up the image of a radical Black Republican. Evidently, such language sold well in the South. By mid-summer, talk of Southern secession if Lincoln were elected was commonplace. Lincoln himself took none of this chatter seriously: he thought it to be nothing more than the usual political sensationalism.

Lincoln in 1860

Nevertheless, the election of 1860 was held under extraordinary circumstances, and the results were equally unprecedented. Four candidates competed, and each of the candidates won some electoral votes. While the Republicans nominated Abraham Lincoln, the Democrats nominated Stephen Douglas, the Southern Democrats chose John C. Breckinridge and the Constitutional Union Party selected John Bell of Tennessee as its nominee. The Constitutional Union Party was compromised of former Know-Nothings and Whigs in the middle states of Kentucky, Tennessee and Virginia who advocated compromise and unity on the issue of slavery.

The race was so fractured that Lincoln only appeared on the ballot in five slave states: Virginia, Kentucky, Maryland, Delaware and Missouri. In Virginia, Lincoln only won about 1% of the vote, and in all the other slave states where Lincoln was on the ballot he finished no better than third. Lincoln won only two counties out all 996 counties in the 15 slave states.

On election night, Lincoln and the Republicans won decisively in the Electoral College, with 180 of the 303 votes cast and 152 needed for a majority. In the popular vote, however, Lincoln only garnered 39%, but came out nearly half a million votes ahead of his next nearest competitor, Stephen Douglas. In the Electoral College, Douglas only won 12 votes with a single state – Missouri. Lincoln swept the North, Breckinridge took the South, and Bell won most of the middle. The results reflected the great regional divide: the nation was set for Civil War.

Chapter 3: 1864
With Lincoln's election on November 6th, 1860, the South was furious. Someone they knew as a "Black Republican" was now set to be inaugurated as President in March. Hate mail streamed into Lincoln's office in Springfield. Never before had a President-elect been received with such malignancy. With death threats hanging over the president-elect, Lincoln was famously hurried through Baltimore by rail into Washington D.C., partly in disguise, to avoid any potential plots.

The press got wind of it and sensationalized the account, giving Lincoln a political black eye before he had even taken office. But this, however, would prove to be a minor problem amid the troubles that lay ahead.

Throughout the fall and winter of 1860, Southern calls for secession became increasingly serious. In a last-ditched effort to save the Union, Kentucky's Senator John Crittenden tried to assume the stateliness of his predecessor Henry Clay. Crittenden, however, proved to be no Henry Clay: his proposal that a Constitutional Amendment reinstate the Missouri Compromise line and extend it to the Pacific failed. President Buchanan supported the measure, but President-Elect Lincoln said he refused to allow the further expansion of slavery under any conditions.

The Crittenden Compromise failed on December 18. Two days later, South Carolina seceded from the Union. President Buchanan sat on his hands, believing the Southern states had no right to secede, but that the Federal government had no effective power to prevent secession. In January, Mississippi, Florida, Alabama, Georgia, Louisiana and Kansas followed South Carolina's lead. The Confederate States of America (CSA) was formed on February 4th, in Montgomery, Alabama, with former Secretary of War Jefferson Davis as its President. On February 23rd, Texas joined the CSA.

Abraham Lincoln hadn't yet assumed office, and yet he had an unprecedented crisis on his hands. Today, Lincoln is remembered as his country's greatest President, but he began his presidency as its least popular ever.

Failing to secure the capture of any major northern cities, or the recognition of Great Britain or France, or the complete destruction of any northern armies, the Confederacy's last chance to survive the Civil War was the election of 1864. Democrats had been pushing an anti-war stance or at least a stance calling for a negotiated peace for years, so the South hoped that if a Democrat defeated President Lincoln, or if anti-war Democrats could retake the Congress, the North might negotiate peace with the South. In the election of 1862, anti-war Democrats made some gains in Congress and won the governorship of the State of New York. Confederates were therefore hopeful that trend would continue to the election of 1864.

Lincoln's reelection was still well in doubt during the summer of 1864. The Democrats nominated George McClellan, the former leader of the Army of the Potomac. McClellan had not been as aggressive as Lincoln hoped, but he was still exceedingly popular with Northern soldiers despite being fired twice, and the Democrats assumed that would make him a tough candidate against Lincon. But right from the start, McClellan was not on the same page with the Democrats, who were divided between those in favor of continuing the war and those who wanted to negotiate a peace with the Confederacy. The compromise was to nominate McClellan, who was in favor of the war, for president, and a vice-presidential candidate who opposed the war.

Furthermore, in the summer of 1864, radical Republicans were still unsure of their support for Lincoln, and many begun running their own campaign against Lincoln for not prosecuting the war vigorously enough, urging Lincoln to withdraw from the campaign. And Lincoln's attempt to break the stalemate in the East by bringing Grant to face Lee only provided a deadlier stalemate during the Overland Campaign.

Instead, it would be the scourge of the South who saved the day. With Grant in the East, control of the Western theater was turned over to William Tecumseh Sherman, who beat back Joseph E. Johnston and John Bell Hood in the Atlanta campaign, taking the important Southern city in early September. On September 3, 1864, Sherman telegrammed Lincoln, "Atlanta is ours and fairly won."

Accordingly, the Republicans renominated Lincoln for the Presidency, but 1864 saw a strange twist in American political history when members of the Democratic Party who had refused to go along with secession joined their Republican counterparts in what was known that year as the "National Union Convention." "1. Resolved, That it is the highest duty of every American citizen to maintain against all their enemies the integrity of the Union and the paramount authority of the Constitution and laws of the United States; and that, laying aside all differences of political opinion, we pledge ourselves, as Union men, animated by a common sentiment and aiming at a common object, to do everything in our power to aid the Government in quelling by force of arms the Rebellion now raging against its authority, and in bringing to the punishment due to their crimes the Rebels and traitors arrayed against it.

"2. Resolved, That we approve the determination of the Government of the United States not to compromise with Rebels, or to offer them any terms of peace, except such as may be based upon an unconditional surrender of their hostility and a return to their just allegiance to the Constitution and laws of the United States, and that we call upon the Government to maintain this position and to prosecute the war with the utmost possible vigor to the complete suppression of the Rebellion, in full reliance upon the self-sacrificing patriotism, the heroic valor and the undying devotion of the American people to the country and its free institutions.

"3. Resolved, That as slavery was the cause, and now constitutes the strength of this Rebellion, and as it must be, always and everywhere, hostile to the principles of Republican Government, justice and the National safety demand its utter and complete extirpation from the soil of the Republic; and that, while we uphold and maintain the acts and proclamations by which the Government, in its own defense, has aimed a deathblow at this gigantic evil, we are in favor, furthermore, of such an amendment to the Constitution, to be made by the people in conformity with its provisions, as shall terminate and forever prohibit the existence of Slavery within the limits of the jurisdiction of the United States."

Looking forward to a reunited Union, the Republican Party made an unprecedented move by nominating a Democrat, Andrew Johnson, for Vice President. Senator Andrew Johnson was notable for being the only Senator to remain loyal to the Union even when his state, Tennessee, had seceded. At the time, the Vice Presidential nomination seemed only a token of goodwill. Little did Republicans know what would happen the following April.

Banner from the 1864 Republican National Convention

Lincoln was solidly reelected in 1864, even winning the military vote against McClellan. He carried all states still loyal to the Union except Kentucky, Delaware and New Jersey. This amounted to an Electoral College vote of 212, against McClellan's 21. In the popular vote, Lincoln beat McClellan by over 400,000 votes.

Chapter 4: Reconstruction

"The war ended in April, 1865, by the fall of Richmond, April 2, and the surrender of General Lee at Appomattox Court House, April 9. The assassination of President Lincoln followed on April 14, and Andrew Johnson became President. It is unnecessary to refer here to his career as President, except to say that his previous bitterness toward those who had been in rebellion against the government changed entirely, and his course' toward congress in the reconstruction of the Southern states was of such a hostile nature as to delay the pacification of the country, and his attitude toward secretary Stanton and General Grant, then general of the army, brought about his impeachment, which failed on account of a few Republican senators voting with Democratic senators for his acquittal. Meanwhile, General Grant retained the love and affection of the people, as the ablest and most successful general of the war. His great modesty was proverbial, and he had shown much executive ability in all matters coming before him. As 1868 approached, he was the man most talked of and written about, as the next candidate of the Republican party for President, and when the convention assembled on May 20, in Chicago, no other name was mentioned. It was, indeed, an interesting convention, and attended from the different states by their ablest men as delegates."

In his second inaugural address, considered perhaps America's greatest speech, Lincoln struck a conciliatory tone, reminding both sides that they prayed to the same God for victory and that neither side could divine God's will. "With malice toward none and charity for all", Lincoln called for peace and reunion, his eye clearly on Reconstruction.

With this clear mandate for governing, the Republicans in the House, with Lincoln's support, approved of the 13th Amendment to the Constitution, which banned slavery in all territories and states. To assist freed slaves, Congress also created the Freedmen's Bureau, to offer food, clothing and shelter to former slaves in the South. Lincoln did his part as well, issuing a Proclamation for Amnesty and Reconstruction, which offered full pardons and amnesty to all Rebels, except those high level officials involved in governing the Confederacy.

In Lincoln's mind, because the South had never legally seceded, forgiveness was to be his top priority. He wanted to allow states to be readmitted to the Union after only 10% of its citizens swore an oath of loyalty to the United States. This was known as the 10% Plan. Congress, now run by the so-called "Radical Republicans," disagreed. As early as the summer of 1864, Congress passed the Wade-Davis Bill, which required 50% of rebel states to swear an oath, not 10%. Lincoln vetoed the bill.

Lincoln envisioned a relatively short-lived Reconstruction process in which the former Confederate states would draft constitutions and rejoin the Union. He thought the country could effectively continue operating much as it had before the War. Lincoln's vision, however, would remain just a dream, when his life, and thus his role in Reconstruction, was cut short just days after Appomattox.

Lincoln in March 1865

With the Civil War near its end and the need for Reconstruction or reconciliation to begin, the North was without its leader. It would fall on a Southerner, Andrew Johnson, to guide the United States into the post-Civil War era.

To say that Andrew Johnson had a rocky presidency would be an understatement, as he was the first president to be impeached and came within a vote of being convicted. One of the men caught in the middle of the bitter conflict between President Johnson and the group of congressmen known as the Radical Republicans was Union war hero Ulysses S. Grant. The "Radicals" demanded harsh treatment of the former "enemies of the state" but strict protection of the rights of the Blacks. Johnson planned to make an example of Robert E. Lee in particular by making him stand trial for treason, but he wanted to institute policies that restricted Blacks' rights. Grant stepped forward to remind Johnson of the terms of the surrender at Appomattox, impressing upon him that it was time to let the nation mend. Grant also opposed Johnson's interference with military commanders sent into the South to carry out Reconstruction policies, and he let his sentiment known.

Johnson

Grant

In July of 1867, President Johnson informed Grant that he intended to remove Edward M. Stanton as the Secretary of War in order to test the constitutionality of the Tenure of Office Act, passed by congressional Republicans, requiring Congressional approval for such removals from office. On August 12, Grant was ordered to serve as Secretary *ad interim*. When Congress convened in January of 1868 and demanded that Stanton be reinstated, Grant relinquished the office, infuriating Johnson, and effectively cementing Grant's ties to the Republican Party.

Given the assassination of Lincoln and the Johnson presidency, it was a sad and divided convention that met in 1868 to try to carry out the wishes of their first successful candidate, now a martyred president. The members began their platform on an optimistic note: "First—We congratulate the country on the assured success of the reconstruction policy of Congress, as evinced by the adoption, in the majority of the States lately in rebellion, of constitutions securing equal civil and political rights to all, and regard it as the duty of the Government to sustain those constitutions, and to prevent the people of such States from being remitted to a state of anarchy or military rule. Second—The guaranty by Congress of equal suffrage to all loyal men at the South was demanded by every consideration of public safety, of gratitude, and of justice, and must be maintained; while the question of suffrage in all the loyal States properly belongs to the people of those States."

Having dismissed with the pleasantries, as one might say, the men moved on to make the astonishing move of castigating Johnson. The platform declared, "Third—We denounce all forms of repudiation as a national crime; and national honor requires the payment of the public indebtedness in the utmost good faith to all creditors at home and abroad, not only according to the letter, but the spirit of the laws under which it was contracted. … Fifth—The National Debt, contracted as it has been for the preservation of the Union for all time to come, should be extended over a fair period of redemption, and it is the duty of Congress to reduce the rate of interest thereon whenever it can be done honestly. Sixth—That the best policy to diminish our burden of debt, is to so improve our credit that capitalists will seek to loan us money at lower rates of interest than we now pay and must continue to pay so long as repudiation, partial or total, open or covert, is threatened or suspected. Seventh—The Government of the United States should be administered with the strictest economy; and the corruptions which have been so shamefully nursed and fostered by Andrew Johnson call loudly for radical reform."

In the same vein, the convention subsequently moved on to deal with the tragedy that was still on everyone's mind: "Eighth—We profoundly deplore the untimely and tragic death of Abraham Lincoln, and regret the accession of Andrew Johnson to the Presidency, who has acted treacherously to the people who elected him and the cause he was pledged to support; has usurped high legislative and judicial functions; has refused to execute the laws; has used his high office to induce other officers to ignore and violate the laws; has employed his executive powers to render insecure the property, the peace, the liberty, and life of the citizen; has abused the pardoning power; has denounced the National Legislature as unconstitutional; has persistently and corruptly resisted, by every means in his power, every proper attempt at the reconstruction of the States lately in rebellion; has perverted the public patronage into an engine of wholesale corruption; and has been justly impeached for high crimes and misdemeanors, and properly pronounced guilty thereof by the vote of thirty-five senators."

At the Republican National Convention, held in Chicago on May 21, 1868, Grant was nominated almost unanimously to be the party's candidate for president. In his acceptance letter to the Republican Election Committee, Grant ended with the statement, "Let us have peace", which became the Republican campaign slogan.

1868 Convention Poster

In the Election of 1868, Grant emerged with a popular majority vote over the Democratic opponent, former New York State Governor Horatio Seymour, winning only by 306,000 votes out of a total 5,715,000 cast. Surprisingly enough, Grant was the first West Point graduate to become President of the United States. While the issue hadn't been considered prior to the election, the marginal win reflected the precarious state of the nation and the need for the Republicans to reassert control over the South if peace was to become a reality.

Taking office on March 4, 1869 at the age of 46, Grant became the 18th president of the United States, the youngest elected president, and the least politically experienced; he'd never held public office and had voted only once in his life, for Democrat James Buchanan in 1856. In his inaugural address, the new president, a man more accustomed to giving orders than giving speeches, gave a less than inspiring oration: "Your suffrages having elected me to the office of President of the United States, I have, in conformity to the Constitution of our country, taken the oath of office prescribed therein. I have taken this oath without mental reservation and with the determination to do to the best of my ability all that is required of me. The responsibilities of the position I feel, but accept them without fear. The office has come to me unsought; I commence its duties untrammeled. I bring to it a conscious desire and determination to fill it to the best of my ability to the satisfaction of the people. On all leading questions agitating the public mind I will always express my views to Congress and urge them according to my judgment, and when I think it advisable will exercise the constitutional privilege of interposing a veto to defeat measures which I oppose; but all laws will be faithfully executed, whether they meet my approval or not. I shall on all subjects have a policy to recommend, but none to enforce against the will of the people. Laws are to govern all alike--those opposed as well as those who favor them. I know no method to secure the repeal of bad or obnoxious laws so effective as their stringent execution."

Grant's speech was just the beginning of his problems. His term was scarred by scandal, and in 1872 a small group of Republicans broke away from the larger party and formed the Liberal Republican Party, nominating for their candidate the popular journalist Horace Greeley. But many knew from the start that while Greeley was a respected journalist, his radical views on most social issues were far too extreme for even Grant's critics. And truth be told, it was widely known that the Democrats were even more corrupt than they were accusing the Grant Administration of being. In several big cities, most notoriously the Tammany Hall machine in New York City, their political machines were actively swindling taxpayers of millions of dollars, and many knew it. And the ace up the Republican's sleeve was, of course, the new Black vote in the South, which they were certain to draw. Thus, Grant won his party's bid for reelection and took more than 66% of the popular vote in the Election of 1872, an even wider margin than in 1868.

In response to the Liberal Republicans, those remaining issued a platform that began by reminding the public of what the party had done for the nation: "During eleven years of supremacy it has accepted with grand courage the solemn duties of the time. It suppressed a gigantic rebellion, emancipated four millions of slaves, decreed the equal citizenship of all, and established universal suffrage. Exhibiting unparalleled magnanimity, it criminally punished no man for political offenses, and warmly welcomed all who proved loyalty by obeying the laws and dealing justly with their neighbors. It has steadily decreased with firm hand the resultant disorders of a great war, and initiated a wise and humane policy toward the Indians. The Pacific railroad and similar vast enterprises have been generously aided and successfully conducted, the public lands freely given to actual settlers, immigration protected and encouraged, and a full acknowledgment of the naturalized citizens' rights secured from European Powers. A uniform national currency has been provided, repudiation frowned down, the national credit sustained under the most extraordinary burdens, and new bonds negotiated at lower rates. The revenues have been carefully collected and honestly applied. Despite large annual reductions of the rates of taxation, the public debt has been reduced during General Grant's Presidency at the rate of a hundred millions a year, great financial crises have been avoided, and peace and plenty prevail throughout the land. Menacing foreign difficulties have been peacefully and honorably composed, and the honor and power of the nation kept in high respect throughout the world. This glorious record of the past is the party's best pledge for the future. We believe the people will not intrust the Government to any party or combination of men composed chiefly of those who have resisted every step of this beneficent progress."

As soon as Grant began his second term, he had to initiate damage control due to a scandal that had begun during his reelection campaign and greatly undermined Republican Party credibility. It had been discovered that several high-ranking Republican officials, including Vice President

Schuyler Colfax and Vice President replacement nominee Senator Henry Wilson, were part of a fraud scheme involving the Union Pacific Railroad and the Crédit Mobilier of America construction company, and had illegally netted a reported 50,000,000 through a clever scheme involving cash bribes to congressmen. And though Crédit Mobilier had been formed in 1864 (during Abraham Lincoln's presidency), and the actual fraud had taken place during the Andrew Johnson presidency in 1868, the public revelation during Grant's presidency made it his mess to clean up.

Although Grant would never be personally accused of wrongdoing during his presidency, ultimately his Administration is best remembered for rampant graft and corruption. In 1875, Secretary of Treasury Benjamin H. Bristow exposed the "Whisky Ring," an operation with roots in the U. S. government, tied to several government officials conspiring with tax officials to rob the government of excise tax. Implicated in the conspiracy was President Grant's own private secretary, General Orville E. Babcock.

Then in 1876, Grant made the reckless decision to allow Secretary of War William W. Belknap to tender his letter of resignation the same day he was to face impeachment for accepting bribes from an Indian agent. Although Belknap was still impeached, it reflected very badly on Grant. And just before the Republican National Convention of 1876, rumors began to spread about a suspicious connection between the Union Pacific Railroad and former Speaker of the House, James G. Blaine.

In short, Grant's second term in office was characterized by a series of scandals and cover-ups, with his many accomplishments buried beneath shame and suspicion. Even today, history tends to forget that in April of 1874 it was Grant's wise veto of the Greenback bill that resulted in diminishing the currency crisis of the final decades of the 19th century, and that his lenient Reconstruction policy did much to reunite the nation.

In his final address to Congress before leaving office, Grant assured them, "Failures have been errors of judgment, not of intent."[1]

Chapter 5: The Election of 1876

"The seventh Republican National Convention assembled in Chicago in June, 1880. Rutherford B. Hayes had been inaugurated as President March 5, 1877 (the 4th coming on Sunday). In his inaugural address he substantially restated the principles and views of policy set forth in his letter of acceptance. … His course toward the South was conciliatory and resulted in establishing peace in South Carolina and Louisiana, where there were rival state governments. A commission was sent to the latter state composed of eminent men of both parties…. Their mission was a successful one. The administration of President Hayes, although attacked by politicians of both

---

[1]   *PBS, American Experience*, "Timeline: Ulysses S. Grant."

parties, was on the whole very satisfactory to the people at large. By withdrawing the federal troops from the southern state houses, and restoring to the people of those states practical self-government, it prepared the way for that revival of patriotism among those lately estranged from the Union; that fraternal feeling between the two sections of the country, and the wonderful material advancement of the South. It conducted with wisdom and firmness, the preparations for the resumption of specie payments, as well as the funding of the public debt at lower rates of interest, and thus facilitated the development of the remarkable business prosperity that continued to its close." – Tweedy

It seems that every time a presidential election rolls around in America, voters are told that the nation is at a critical fork in its history, and that the decisions reached and the candidates elected will change the course of history. While this is always true to some extent, there are times when it is true to a critical extent. Such was the case in 1876, when the country, weary of four years of Civil War and more than a decade of Reconstruction, was once again on the brink of splitting. While the Northern states celebrated the centennial of American Independence, the South found itself chaffing under the weight of federal occupation. At the same time, the entire nation was shocked and horrified at the direction the Indian Wars in the West were going, culminating just weeks before the election with George Custer's shocking defeat at the Battle of the Little Bighorn.

At the same time, Southern politicians were beginning to make a comeback and the Democratic Party was gaining strength, especially in the former Confederate states. The South hoped that if it could once again win the White House, it could finally resume its position as an equal part of the nation, rather than a section being punished for its past.

All of this set the stage for one of the strangest interludes in American history. As the nation's two major parties each put forth a large slate of candidates for nomination, two candidates had to come to the fore, and each party selected both a presidential and vice-presidential candidate. These four men ran a bitterly contested race just to reach the general election, and that general election became the most controversial in American history.

As anyone who has watched the Republican primaries unfold in 2016 knows, more candidates can create more chaos, and this was especially true in 1876, when a total of 9 candidates sought the Republican Party's nomination. Among these men was William A. Wheeler, a New York Congressman who had served in Congress off and on since before the Civil War. Nearly a century later, he earned a mention in *Profiles in Courage* by Senator John F. Kennedy.

Wheeler

Wheeler knew that he did have a shot if he could compete successfully against Senator James G. Blaine of Maine. There were, of course, other candidates who hoped to have some sort of chance against Blaine, or at least have the honor of being nominated. Benjamin Bristow of Kentucky resigned from his position as the Secretary of the Treasury under Grant to run, billing himself as a reformer who would clean up the White House scandals that surrounded Grant's administration.

Bristow

Blaine

Last but far from least was Rutherford B. Hayes, a man whom Perley described as "one of the purest public men of the day, and aside from possessing remarkable personal influence, he has brilliant abilities and has had a larger and varied experience in public life, both civil and military." With his excellent war record, Hayes was practically a sure bet for nearly any political office he wanted.

By the time the Republicans met for their National Convention in Cincinnati, Ohio, it was obvious that there was going to be trouble. Even after the men had had time to meet and talk and debate, tensions still ran high. The *Janesville Gazette* in nearby Wisconsin reported on the controversy surrounding the seventh and final ballot, taken on June 17:

> "Immediately after the call began a delegate from New York said: I move we take a recess of ten minutes. [Cries of "no; no."]

> "The Chair—The point of order is made that the calling of the roll having been commenced, the motion for a recess is not in order.

"Mr. Edick—I ask permission for the New York delegation to withdraw.

"The Chair—If the New York delegation desires to withdraw, they can do it at their own motion, without addressing the chair.

"Immediately after Colorado was called the New York delegation withdrew, following the example set by the Pennsylvanians. Just after Colorado had been called, a delegate from Virginia arose and said: "There are gents on the floor who do not belong to the convention. I insist upon their being removed." There was no necessity for exertion on the part of the sergeant-at-arms, as the outsiders quietly walked from among the delegates. At this moment the New York delegation began to withdraw to an anti-room for consultation.

"Mr. Rogers, of New York—I ask unanimous consent that all be suspended until the delegations which desire to do so can retire and return.

"Cries of 'No,' 'No,' and 'Yes,' 'Yes.'

"The Chair—It requires unanimous consent to suspend the calling of the roll.

"Several delegates made the motion.

"Mr. Ambler,.of Ohio—I move that a recess be taken for fifteen minutes to allow the delegations time to cousult. The Chair—It is not in order to make that motion pending the roll call. [Confusion.]

"Mr. Ambler—I move to suspend rules.

"The Chair—That motion nor any other is not in order while the roll is being culled. [Disorder.]"

By this time, it was clear Hayes would eventually get the nomination, but many were unhappy about it. The article continued:

"The change of Mississippi to Hayes provoked another outburst of yells. When New York was called Mr. Pomeroy said: "To indicate that Now York is in favor of unity and victory she calls 61 votes for Rutherford B. Hayes and nine votes for James Blaine." This result was greeted by furious cheers. When Montana was called the chairman said: "Montana, yielding to none in admiration of the gallant statesman from Maine, casts 2 votes for Rutherford B Hayes." The result of the vote was known as soon as the roll-call was over, and the delegates on the victorious side abandoned themselves to shouts of triumph.

"The Chair—The vote is as follows: Total number of votes, 750 necessary to a choice; 371, Hayes; 384 [furious and continued applause, which drowned the music of the band] Blaine; 351, Bristow. Rutherford B. Hayes of the state of Ohio, having received a majority of all the votes cast, is hereby declared to be the nominee of this convention for the office of president of the United States. It is moved that the nomination of the convention be made unanimous, and on that Mr. Frye, of Maine, has the floor.

"Mr. Frye, of Maine—Mr. President, I know, sir, that this immense and enthusiastic convention will pardon me if I say just one word of kindness and of thanks to the glorious supporters that our candidate, Mr. Blaine, has had here. No words of mine can express the thanks which Maine gives to you men who have stood by her as you have here to-day. God bless you forever and ever. … We recognize the fact that the convention in its wisdom has selected the Hon. Mr. Hayes as the standard-bearer in this next great contest for liberty, for justice, for humanity, and for civilization, and the state of Maine accepts and endorses fully and completely and rejoices in the nomination of Mr. Hayes."

Next, the party spent a bit of time voting on the Vice-Presidential candidate until choosing William A. Wheeler.

From this point, the group moved on to the all-important issue of the party's platform for the election. Once the platform had been decided, it began, "When in the economy of Providence this land was to be purged of human slavery, and when the strength of the government of the people, by the people, for the people, was to be demonstrated, the Republican Party came into power. Its deeds have passed into history, and we look back to them with pride incited by their memories, and high aims for the good of our country and mankind; and, looking to the future with unfaltering courage, hope, and purpose, we, the representatives of the party in national convention assembled, make the following declaration of principles."

The platform then went on to revisit what was still considered the most important issue of the day: how to deal with the South. The first three points said:

"1. The United States of America is a nation, not a league. By the combined workings of the national and state governments under their respective constitutions, the rights of every citizen are secured at home and protected abroad, and the common welfare promoted.

"2. The republican party his preserved those governments to their hundredth anniversary of the nation's birth, and they are now embodiments of the great truths spoken at its cradle, that 'all men are created equal;' that they are 'endowed by their Creator with certain inalienable rights, among which are life, liberty, and the pursuit of happiness; that, for the attainment of those ends, governments have been instituted among men, deriving their just powers from the consent of the governed.' Until these truths are cheerfully obeyed, or it need be, vigorously enforced, the work of the Republican Party is unfinished.

"3. The permanent pacification of the southern section of the Union, and the complete protection of its citizens the free enjoyment of all their rights, are duties to which the Republican Party stands sacredly pledged. The power to provide for the enforcement of the principles embodied in the recent constitutional amendments is vested by those amendments in the congress of the United States; and we declare it to be the solemn obligation of the legislative and executive departments of the government to put into immediate and vigorous exercise in their constitutional powers for removing any just causes of discontent on the part of any class, and for securing to every American citizen complete liberty and exact equality in the exercise of all civil, political and public rights. To this end we imperatively demand a congress and a chief executive whose courage and fidelity to these duties shall not falter until these results are placed beyond dispute or recall."

The platform then went on to deal (albeit discreetly) with the issue of the corruption that plagued the recent administration: "The invariable rule for appointments should have reference to the honesty, fidelity, and capacity of the appointee, giving to the party in power those places where harmony and vigor of administration requires its policy to be represented, but permitting all others to be filled by persons selected with sole reference to the efficiency of the public service, and the right of all citizens to share in the honor of rendering faithful service to their country…We rejoice in the quickened conscience of the people concerning political affairs and will hold all officers to a rigid responsibility, and engage that the prosecution and punishment of all who betray official trusts shall be speedy, thorough, and unsparing."

A Republican campaign poster

A contemporary sketch of the hall at the moment Hayes was nominated

As if determined not to be outdone by the Republicans, the Democrats had nearly as many men seeking their party's nomination as their political counterparts did. From the beginning, the leader of the group was Samuel J. Tilden, then the Governor of New York. In 1889, Hugh Mcculloch, who had served as the Secretary of the Treasury in the administrations of presidents Lincoln, Johnson, and Arthur, called Tilden "a man of distinguished ability in his profession." There were also a number of procedural differences between the Republican and Democratic Conventions, the most obvious being that the Democrats voted on their party platform before nominating its candidates.

It's fair to say that no one who was in touch with the national situation believed that the Election of 1876 was going to go smoothly. It was common knowledge that fraud was rampant across the nation, with both parties pulling out every trick in the book to get their way. People who had been dead for years managed to "vote," while those who were alive were turned away from the polls if they were not deemed worthy of being able to cast a ballot. These were problems that plagued regular elections, so there was little hope that the one held on November 7, 1876 would be any different.

At the end of Election Day, it was clear that Tilden had carried the popular vote. On November

8, the *Galveston Gazette* reported, "Unless there is some radical error in the indication of figures thus far received, the election of Tilden and Hendricks may be claimed with absolute certainly. The total electoral vote is 369, and 185 are required to elect. In Democratic estimation before the election as many as 205 voted were set down to the Tilden column, and 184 in the Hayes column. This made the possibility of Hayes's election depend on his getting the thirty-five votes of New York, not conceded to him, or twenty-one or more votes from other States claimed by the Democrats. Hence New York becomes the chief battle ground towards the close of the canvass, and the loss of that State by the Republicans may be laid to have decided the general result for Tilden. The occasion is one for joy and congratulation beyond the power of words. The good sense and the intelligent patriotism of the American people have once more prevailed. The country is redeemed—the future of this republic is safe."

However, the joy of the editors of the *Galveston Gazette* and other Democratic papers was short lived, because immediately below that story was a last minute addition that stifled everyone's early hopes: "3 A.M.—Northern Republicans concede 184 electoral votes to Tilden, claiming, Florida, Louisiana, Nevada, Oregon and South Carolina as doubtful, any one of which States would secure Tilden's election."

Ben Perley captured the mood of the capital shortly after the election results began to come in, and just how unprecedented the situation was: "Washington was wild with excitement immediately after the Presidential election. The returns received late on Tuesday night indicated the election of Mr. Tilden, and even the Republican newspapers announced on the following morning the result as doubtful. Senator Chandler, who was at New York, was the only confident Republican, and he telegraphed to the Capitol, 'Hayes has one hundred and eighty-five votes and is elected.' He also telegraphed to President Grant recommending the concentration of United States troops at the Southern capitals to insure a fair count. President Grant at once ordered General Sherman to instruct the commanding generals in Louisiana and Florida to be vigilant with the forces at their command to preserve peace and good order, and to see that the proper and legal boards of canvassers were unmolested in the performance of their duties. 'Should there be,' said he, 'any grounds of suspicion of fraudulent count on either side, it should be reported and denounced at once. No man worthy of the office of President should be willing to hold it if counted in or placed there by fraud. Either party can afford to be disappointed by the result. The country cannot afford to have the result tainted by the suspicion of illegal or false returns.'"

Oregon and Nevada were quickly decided for Hayes, giving him 166 electoral votes, but the three Southern States hung in the balance. By this time, there had been so much fraud and intimidation exercised by both parties that there was really no way of knowing what the honest totals were. Intent on making sure that the vote count in South Carolina, Louisiana, and Florida was accurate and untainted by Democratic Party intimidation, the Republicans set up "returning boards" to oversee the recounts of ballots.

Needless to say, the stakes could not have been higher; Hayes needed all 19 electoral votes from those states, while Tilden was only one elector away from the presidency. Perhaps not surprisingly, the results from the returning boards only inflamed the issue when all three states were awarded to Hayes, with the Republican being declared the winner.

Louisiana's unofficial tallies had shown Tilden the winner by some 6,000 votes, but the Republican controlled returning board threw out 15,000 due to allegations of fraud and voter intimidation, giving the state's 8 electoral votes to Hayes. In South Carolina, the same scenario worked itself out, with enough votes being thrown out that the state went for Hayes, along with nullifying the victories of the Democratic gubernatorial candidate and Democratic legislators. In both states, the Democrats set up rival state governments (each with their own governors and legislature) and awarded the state's electoral votes to Tilden.

In Florida, the state that subsequently played a central role in the contested election of 2000, the situation was even more complicated. The first vote tallies showed Hayes the victor by just 43 votes, but a recount had Tilden victorious by 94 votes. The Republican controlled returning board disallowed enough ballots to deliver the state to Hayes by about 1,000 votes, and this action, as it had in Louisiana and South Carolina, had the added effect of overturning the gubernatorial result and awarding the office to the Republican candidate. Further complicating the situation, the Florida Supreme Court threw out these results and awarded the governorship to Democrat George Franklin Drew, who promptly announced that Tilden and not Hayes had won Florida.

Drew

   In addition to those ongoing controversies, there was a relatively minor dispute in Oregon. Unlike in the three Southern states, Hayes' victory was not in question, but Democrats did, however, question the eligibility of one of Hayes' electors, John W. Watts. At the time of the election, Watts was a United States postmaster, a position he resigned from a week after the election and long before the electors met. The Democrats nevertheless argued that Watts was constitutionally ineligible to serve as an elector because of the Constitution provided that "no…person holding an office of trust or profit under the United States shall be appointed an elector." As a result, the Democratic Governor of Oregon removed Watts and replaced him with a Tilden supporter.

   Such was the state of play when the electors met in their respective state capitals on December 6, 1876 to formally cast their ballots for the presidency. In Florida, South Carolina, and Louisiana, both the Democratic and Republican electors met and cast conflicting votes. In Oregon, both the Hayes and Tilden supporter cast a ballot. Thus, at the end of the day, four states forwarded two sets of returns to Washington to be opened by the House of Representatives.

   The unique way the Founders settled on choosing the President, one in which voters cast ballots not directly for President but for the electors who represented their votes for President via the Electoral College, usually worked well (aside from a hiccup in the Election of 1800 that allowed Aaron Burr, who was intended to be Thomas Jefferson's vice president, the ability to challenge Jefferson for the presidency since both were awarded the same number of electors). Although the Electoral College seems archaic now more than ever, the candidate who wins the popular vote almost always won a majority of the electoral votes. On very rare occasions, however, the popular vote winner did not win an electoral majority; but while such circumstances invariably lead to calls to abolish the Electoral College in favor of direct popular voting for the presidency, the legitimacy of the election was almost never called into question until 1876.

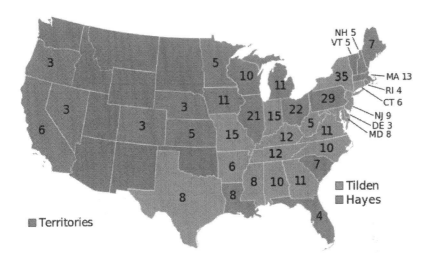

The official results of the Electoral College in 1876

By the time the electors met, it was clear that the Republic faced a situation never seen before. Tilden had won the popular vote by some 250,000 votes, but he did not have a clear electoral majority, having received 184 electors (one short of the 185 needed to have a majority). Meanwhile, Hayes received 165 electoral votes, leaving 20 votes in dispute. The country was facing a constitutional crisis not seen since the end of 1860, and unfortunately, the Constitution provided no clear solution.

In the end, those in charge agreed that an electoral commission was "the best bad plan" they had. On February 2, 1877, *Harper's Weekly* published a report from the United States Congress that concluded, "The unfortunate circumstance that no provision had been made on the subject before the election has greatly added to the difficulty in dealing with it, inasmuch as many of the people of the country, members of the respective political parties, will, perhaps, look with jealousy upon any measure that seems to involve even the probability of the defeat of their wishes, but it has led the committee to feel that their members are bound by the highest duty in such a case to let no bias or party feeling stand in the way of a just, equal, and peaceful measure for extricating the question from the embarrassments that at present surround it. ...we respectfully beg leave to impress upon Congress the necessity of a speedy determination upon this subject. It is impossible to estimate the material loss the country daily sustains from the existing state of uncertainty. It directly and powerfully tends to unsettle and paralyze business, to weaken public and private credit, and to create apprehensions in the minds of the people that disturb the peaceful tenor of their ways and happiness. It does far more -- it tends to bring republican institutions into discredit, and to create doubts of the success of our form of government and of the perpetuity of the republic. All considerations of interest, of patriotism, and of justice unite in demanding of the law-making power a measure that will bring peace and prosperity to the country, and show that our republican institutions are equal to any emergency. And in this connection we can not refrain from expression of our satisfaction that your committee, composed of equal numbers of opposing parties, have fortunately been able to do what has been attempted in vain heretofore -- almost unanimously agree upon a plan considered by them all to be just, wise, and efficient."

Knowing that the entire nation, and indeed the world, was watching, Congress appointed 15 members to the Commission: 5 from the House, 5 from the Senate, and 5 from the Supreme Court. 7 members were Democrats, and the other 8 were Republicans. States were then ordered to send their electoral votes to Washington, knowing that whenever one state submitted two different certificates, the Commission would decide which one to accept. Its decision would be final and could only be challenged by the power of both houses of the United States Congress.

As Ben Perley aptly put it, "The Electoral Commission was a cunningly devised plan for declaring Mr. Hayes legally elected President. In the then feverish condition of parties at the Capitol, with no previously arranged plan for adjusting controverted questions, it was evident that some plan should be devised for a peaceful solution of the difficulty. Republicans conceived the idea of an Electoral Commission, to be composed of five Senators, five Representatives, and five Associate Justices of the Supreme Court. No sooner had Mr. Tilden and his conservative friends agreed to the Commission, in which he would have had one majority, than Judge David Davis, of the Supreme Court, was elected a United States Senator. This made it necessary to select Judge Bradley as the man who was to hold the balance of power. The debate in the Senate on the bill establishing the Electoral Commission was deeply interesting, as several of those who participated were prominent candidates for the Presidency. There was an especial desire to hear Senator Conkling, who had 'sulked in his tent' since the Cincinnati Convention, and the galleries were crowded with noted men and women, diplomats, politicians, soldiers, and journalists from all sections of the Republic."

Not surprisingly, the commission voted 8-7 to accept the Republicans' plan. This precedent continued, and the Commission ended up rewarding all the electoral votes in question to Hayes. The House of Representatives, controlled by the Democrats, voted to overturn those results, but the Republican dominated Senate refused to go along with this and Hayes' election stood.

Whether the end of Reconstruction was brought about by a secret compromise or not, it was certainly the result of Hayes' election. Civil War historian James McPherson noted that the end of Reconstruction ultimately was brought about by the "wavering commitment" of Northern Republicans. Due in part to Southern castigation of Reconstruction, Northern society had become disillusioned with carpetbaggers and was not committed to black rights. The war's "revolutionary achievements" had thus been based more on anti-Southern motivation than pro-black sentiment. To "emancipationist" writers, most notably Frederick Douglass and W.E.B. DuBois, "Reconstruction required a full accounting of the past," an accounting that was not coming in the foreseeable future. Though they appealed to people to remember the necessity of Reconstruction for black Americans, their vision would be obscured in the North out of political expediency.

As for his part, Hayes paid a high price for his win. He was known throughout his presidency by such derisive nicknames as "Rutherfraud" and "His Accidency. The House of Representatives eventually appointed a commission to investigate the outcome, but it was unable to find any clear cut evidence of a conspiracy. Nonetheless, Hayes was almost fatally undermined from the minute he took office, and he would go on to serve one unremarkable term that's best remembered for the election that preceded it.

Chapter 6: Dominance

After the wrangling that landed Hays the presidency, the Republican Party dominated presidential elections for another four decades, largely unchallenged by the still weakened Democrats except for the two terms of Grover Cleveland, the only man who didn't serve his two terms in a row.

The presidencies during the last 20 years of the 19th century were mostly unremarkable, but in 1901, when President William McKinley was assassinated, he was replaced by the young Theodore Roosevelt.

Roosevelt

Thanks to the death of McKinley, Roosevelt had the opportunity to mold the presidency in crucial ways. Roosevelt was able to create the "bully pulpit" of the presidency and ensure that he set the nation's legislative agenda by giving press statements regularly. Every president has since used the office to attempt to determine the nation's legislative priorities.

This personal strengthening of the presidency spilled over into an administrative augmentation of the office of President. Though the Sherman Anti Trust Act had been passed in the 1880s, all presidents before Roosevelt underutilized its power. Roosevelt consolidated much of the power delegated to him by Congress and ensured that the President took an active role in administering the government of the United States. He also expanded the Presidential cabinet and created many new administrative departments, widening the breadth of the nation's federal bureaucracy. Only his fifth cousin, Franklin, would outshine him in this pursuit decades later.

On domestic policy, Theodore Roosevelt's presidency was the height of American progressivism, again outshone only by his distant cousin decades later. Roosevelt brought the ideology of limited, free-market government to its heels and instituted numerous reforms geared towards breaking corporate power and aiding consumers.

Roosevelt's presidency is also credited with making America a global player in international relations. The Panama Canal and the Roosevelt Corollary ensured the U.S. would dominate the Western Hemisphere, and the Portsmouth Treaty also expanded the nation's influence in places it had previously never gone. Roosevelt's expansion of the military and support for an interventionist policy was a marked departure from previous administrations; until Roosevelt, the United States had been rigidly isolationist since Washington offered his neutrality advice as

President.

Thus, it was Roosevelt who ensured the nation would not merely be an economic powerhouse but also participate actively and powerfully in the international sphere. It can safely be said that Roosevelt opened the doors to what would become the "American Century."

Teddy, as he was called, proved to be a boost for the party and was extremely popular with the population. He was elected overwhelmingly to a full term in his own right in 1904, and he remained tremendously popular throughout. That is why it was such a shock when he announced in 1908 that he would not be running for a second full term. Writing in 1910, John Tweedy observed, "In this the greatest era of American advancement the Republican party has reached its highest service under the leader ship of Theodore Roosevelt. His administration is an epoch in American history. In no other period since national sovereignty was won under Washington, or preserved under Lincoln, has there been such mighty progress in those high ideals of government which make for justice, equality and fair dealing among men. The highest aspirations of the American people have found a voice. Their most exalted servant represents the best aims and worthiest purposes of all his countrymen. American manhood has been lifted to a nobler sense of duty and obligation. Conscience and courage in public station and higher standards of right and wrong in private life have become cardinal principles of political faith; capital and labor have been brought into closer relations of confidence and interdependence; and the abuse of wealth, the tyranny of power, and all the evils of privilege and favoritism have been put to scorn by the simple, manly virtues of justice and fair play."

Roosevelt threw his significant political weight behind his good friend and Secretary of State, William Howard Taft, who in his acceptance speech paid tribute to his predecessor: "Mr. Roosevelt has set high the standard of business morality and obedience to law. ... But we should be blind to the ordinary working of human nature if we did not recognize that the moral standards set by President Roosevelt will not continue to be observed by those whom cupidity and a desire for financial power may tempt, unless the requisite machinery is introduced into the law which shall in its practical operation maintain these standards and secure the country against a departure from them. The chief function of the next Administration, in my judgment, is distinct from, and a progressive development of, that which has been performed by President Roosevelt. The chief function of the next Administration is to complete and perfect the machinery by which these standards may be maintained, by which the lawbreakers may be promptly restrained and punished, but which shall operate with sufficient accuracy and dispatch to interfere with legitimate business as little as possible."

Taft went on to win the White House, but his political alliance would not last a full term with Roosevelt, and it had drastic effects in 1912.

By late 1910, Roosevelt revised his opinion on Taft. He wrote Senator Henry Cabot Lodge, saying "I finally had to admit that he [Taft] had gone wrong on certain points; and I then also had to admit to myself that deep down underneath I had all along known he was wrong." Thus, Roosevelt decided to unseat Taft and seek the Presidency himself. Understanding the gravity of his decision, Roosevelt titled this chapter of his autobiography "Armageddon and Afterward."

Roosevelt initially hesitated, however. He opted into the Republican nominating process late in 1911. Regardless, Roosevelt was able to win 9 of the 13 presidential primaries, and it was one of the first times regular citizens got to vote for nominees, but these choices were mostly "beauty contests" that had no control over delegates. The remaining states continued to allow Republican politicians to decide the fate of their delegates. As such, Taft controlled the party's power brokers and was able to narrowly secure the nomination over Roosevelt at the national convention.

Responding to what they considered Roosevelt's betrayal during the convention, the leaders formed a pro-business platform aimed at defeating Roosevelt's "common man" stand. They touched on the subject by saying, "Experience makes it plain that the business of the country may be carried on without fear or without disturbance and at the same time without resort to practices which are abhorrent to the common sense of justice. The Republican party favors the enactment of legislation supplementary to the existing anti-trust act which will define as criminal offences those specific acts that uniformly mark attempts to restrain and to monopolize trade, to the end that those who honestly intend to obey the law may have a guide for their action and those who aim to violate the law may the more surely be punished. The same certainty should be given to the law prohibiting combinations and monopolies that characterize other provisions of commercial law; in order that no part of the field of business opportunity may be restricted by monopoly or combination, that business success honorably achieved may not be converted into crime, and that the right of every man to acquire commodities, and particularly the necessaries of life, in an open market uninfluenced by the manipulation of trust or combination, may be preserved."

From there the convention went on to touch on several key points in American business, specifically:

> "Federal Trade Commission

> "In the enforcement and administration of Federal Laws governing interstate commerce and enterprises impressed with a public use engaged therein, there is much that may be committed to a Federal trade commission, thus placing in the hands of an administrative board many of the functions now necessarily exercised by the courts. This will promote promptness in the administration of the law and avoid delays and technicalities incident to court procedure.

> "The Tariff

"We reaffirm our belief in a protective tariff. The Republican tariff policy has been of the greatest benefit to the country, developing our resources, diversifying our industries, and protecting our workmen against competition with cheaper labor abroad, thus establishing for our wage-earners the American standard of living. The protective tariff is so woven into the fabric of our industrial and agricultural life that to substitute for it a tariff for revenue only would destroy many industries and throw millions of our people out of employment. The products of the farm and of the mine should receive the same measure of protection as other products of American labor.

"We hold that the import duties should be high enough, while yielding a sufficient revenue, to protect adequately American industries and wages. Some of the existing import duties are too high, and should be reduced. Readjustment should be made from time to time to conform to changing conditions and to reduce excessive rates, but without injury to any American industry. To accomplish this correct information is indispensable. This information can best be obtained by an expert commission, as the large volume of useful facts contained in the recent reports of the Tariff Board has demonstrated.

"The pronounced feature of modern industrial life is its enormous diversification. To apply tariff rates justly to these changing conditions requires closer study and more scientific methods than ever before. The Republican party has shown by its creation of a Tariff Board its recognition of this situation, and its determination to be equal to it. We condemn the Democratic party for its failure either to provide funds for the continuance of this board or to make some other provision for securing the information requisite for intelligent tariff legislation. We protest against the Democratic method of legislating on these vitally important subjects without careful investigation.

"We condemn the Democratic tariff bills passed by the House of Representatives of the Sixty-second Congress as sectional, as injurious to the public credit, and as destructive to business enterprise."

A scene from the 1912 Republican National Convention

William Howard Taft

Befriending politicians had never been Roosevelt's strong suit, and Roosevelt thus encountered a problem, but it was one that had always plagued his political life: he was broadly popular with the public but was disdained by his fellow politicians, a dilemma that had brought him to the Vice Presidency in the first place. But the former president didn't give up at this point. Roosevelt took his supporters out of the Republican National Convention in protest and formed his own Progressive Party. When Teddy proclaimed he was "as fit as a bull moose," the party became known as the "Bull Moose Party."

Roosevelt's proposals throughout the nomination fight and the general election were some of his most radical. He railed against the "unholy" alliance of government and corporate interests and accused them of holding a "sinister influence or control of special interests" over national government. As president he was certainly a populist, but as a presidential candidate in 1912 he transformed into the populist's populist.

The former president was now labeled a radical. To this he wrote, "The criticism had been made of me that I am a radical. So I am. I couldn't be anything else, feeling as I do. But I am a radical who most earnestly desires to see the radical programme carried out by conservatives." In his attacks, Roosevelt did not hold back. He openly railed against specific corporations and conglomerates, including Standard Oil and U.S. Steel.

For his own part, Wilson tried to claim the progressive mantle from Roosevelt by touting a progressive agenda in his campaign speeches that became known as the "New Freedom" agenda, which included tariff reform, labor reform and banking reform. To accomplish this, Wilson sought to differentiate himself and Roosevelt by tying Roosevelt's progressivism as more collectivist (and thus socialist) than his progressivism, which he couched as supporting free enterprise: "If America is not to have free enterprise, he can have freedom of no sort whatever."

On October 14th, 1912, Roosevelt's campaign was nearly brought to an unhappy end, albeit one that solidified the Roosevelt legend. Roosevelt was in Milwaukee to deliver a campaign speech when a local barkeep named John Schrank caught wind of Roosevelt's location and shot him as he was leaving a hotel to deliver the speech at the Milwaukee Auditorium. Thankfully, the bullet passed through a folded up copy of Roosevelt's 50 page speech and his eyeglass case before lodging in his ribcage short of his lungs or heart. An adept hunter and something of a scientist, Roosevelt noticed he was not coughing blood and concluded that the bullet must not have penetrated a vital organ. In his typical cowboy-like fashion, Roosevelt refused to go to the hospital and delivered the speech with blood seeping through his shirt. He announced to the audience that he had been shot, saying "it takes more than one bullet to kill a Bull Moose."

John Schrank

Roosevelt went to the hospital shortly after the assassination attempt and remained there for nearly a week. Taft and challenger Woodrow Wilson halted their campaigns in honor of the former president, only resuming them when Roosevelt resumed his. The assassination attempt, however, did not rally the American people around Roosevelt. On Election Day, he came in second behind Wilson, with 27% of the vote, the most a third party candidate had ever won. Incumbent President Taft came in third, making him the first president seeking reelection to lose by coming in third rather than second. However, the split in the Republican Party had handed the presidency to a Democrat. President Wilson was the first two-term Democratic President since before the Civil War.

The Republican Party's plan had worked on one level, in that it denied Roosevelt his sought after return to the White House. On another, more important level, however, it failed miserably, losing the White House to a Democratic opponent for the first time in almost 30 years.

Chapter 7: The Principles and Traditions of Our Party

"We, the representatives of the Republican Party, in convention assembled, renew our pledge to the principles and traditions of our party and dedicate it anew to the service of the nation. We meet in a period of widespread distress and of an economic depression that has swept the world. The emergency is second only to that of a great war. The human suffering occasioned may well exceed that of a period of actual conflict. The supremely important problem that challenges our citizens and government alike is to break the back of the depression, to restore the economic life of the nation and to bring encouragement and relief to the thousands of American families that are sorely afflicted.

"The people themselves, by their own courage, their own patient and resolute effort in the readjustments of their own affairs, can and will work out the cure. It is our task as a party, by leadership and a wise determination of policy, to assist that recovery. To that task we pledge all that our party possesses in capacity, leadership, resourcefulness and ability. Republicans, collectively and individually, in nation and State, hereby enlist in a war which will not end until the promise of American life is once more fulfilled. For nearly three years the world has endured an economic depression of unparalleled extent and severity. The patience and courage of our people have been severely tested, but their faith in themselves, in their institutions and in their future remains unshaken. When victory comes, as it will, this generation will hand on to the next a great heritage unimpaired." – The Republican Party Platform, 1932

1924 proved to be a banner year for the Republican National Convention in a number of ways. It was the first such convention to allow women to participate in the proceedings, in a way fulfilling something the party had pledged 28 years earlier at its 1896 convention: "The Republican party is mindful of the rights and interests of women. Protection of American industries includes equal opportunities, equal pay for equal work, and protection to the home. We favor the admission of women to wider spheres of usefulness, and welcome their co-operation in rescuing the country from Democratic and Populistic mismanagement and misrule." Four years later, in 1900, Frances Warring became the first female delegate to the convention, representing the state of Wyoming. Beginning in 1924, the Republican Party of each state would have both a national committeeman and a national committeewoman.

A crowd outside the 1924 Republican convention

The 1924 Republican National Convention also made history by being the first to be publicly broadcast over radio, though it was only carried in nine cities. The Douglas Radio Company took out a special advertisement reminding people to "Don't Fail To Hear The Republican National Convention BROADCAST BY RADIO; Hear a President and Vice-President nominated. If you have no radio set, Come in and let us fit you." Those tuned in had the rare privilege of hearing a nominee turn down his party's offer when Governor Frank Lowden refused the nomination for Vice-President, saying, "If I am nominated, I will refuse to accept it. So far I have always kept my word to the public when I have given it. I shall do so now. I told the public I was not and would not be a candidate for vice president. I'll not go back on my word. I thank the convention, but I will not accept the nomination." This remains the only time in history when anyone ever refused the Vice-Presidency.

Lowden

Calvin Coolidge, the Republican incumbent in 1924, accepted the Presidential nomination and won a second term easily, opening the door for Herbert Hoover to follow him in 1928. This was a time of prosperity in the nation, and the men writing the platform declared enthusiastically, "The record of the United States Treasury under Secretary Mellon stands unrivalled and unsurpassed. The finances of the nation have been managed with sound judgment. The financial policies have yielded immediate and substantial results. In 1921 the credit of our government was at a low ebb. We were burdened with a huge public debt, a load of war taxes, which in variety and weight exceeded anything in our national life, while vast unfunded intergovernmental debts disorganized the economic life of the debtor nations and seriously affected our own by reason of the serious obstacles which they presented to commercial intercourse. This critical situation was evidenced by a serious disturbance in our own life which made for unemployment. Today all these major financial problems have been solved."

However, within 18 months, the financial bubble that had grown the economy to new heights burst, and Hoover was left with an untenable situation that he could neither fix nor avoid the blame for on his watch. When he reluctantly accepted nomination for the second term in 1932, he told the members of the convention, "The solution of our many problems which arise from the shifting scene of national life is not to be found in haphazard experimentation or by revolution. It must be through organic development of our national life under these ideals. It must secure that cooperative action which brings initiative and strength outside of the Government. It does not follow, because our difficulties are stupendous, because there are some souls timorous enough to doubt the validity and effectiveness of our ideals and our system, that we must turn to a State-controlled or State-directed social or economic system in order to cure our troubles. That is not liberalism; that is tyranny. It is the regimentation of men under autocratic bureaucracy with all its extinction of liberty, of hope, and of opportunity. Of course, no man of understanding says that our system works perfectly. It does not for the human race is not yet perfect. Nevertheless, the movement of true civilization is towards freedom rather than regimentation. And that is our ideal. Oft times the tendency of democracy in the presence of national danger is to strike blindly, to listen to demagogues and to slogans, all of which destroy and do not save. We have refused to be stampeded into such courses. Oft times democracy elsewhere in the world has been unable to move fast enough to save itself in emergency. There have been disheartening delays and failures in legislation and private action which -have added to the losses of our people, yet this democracy of ours has proved its ability to act."

With the economy still cratering, Democrats were yearning for victory in 1932. The Democrats had only won the White House four times since the Civil War, and each time only because of unusual or precarious circumstances. With the Great Depression deepening, the party saw an opening to shift the American political paradigm in its favor.

Many looked to Franklin Roosevelt to carry the banner of change, but not all Democrats were initially convinced. Southern Democrats were especially wary of nominating Roosevelt, ironically because of his supposed pro-Catholic leanings. Roosevelt's early antagonistic relationship with Irish voters in New York belied that belief, and his support of Catholicism had been tepid and political in nature, making it a relatively easy issue for him to surmount. On the fourth ballot at the party's Chicago convention, Roosevelt was selected as the nominee, with Speaker of the House John Nance Garner as his running mate.

Until 1932, tradition dictated that a candidate accept a nomination in writing only. Roosevelt broke this tradition, flew to Chicago, and told the convention "I pledge to you, I pledge to myself, to a new deal for the American people." That phrase would define the first half of his

Presidency.

On Election Day, Roosevelt won handily. In one of the biggest margins in electoral history, Roosevelt carried 472 electoral votes to Hoover's 59, winning 57% of the popular vote to Hoover's 39%. It was an historic victory, indeed. Roosevelt's victory was the first since 1848 in which the Democrats won with a majority of the popular vote, and no president from either party had ever won more electoral votes. Furthermore, the Democrats won substantial majorities in the House and Senate. Thereafter, Democrats would hold a majority in the House for all but four years until 1995. It was, without question, precisely the shift the Democrats had hoped it would be.

Roosevelt would win 4 presidential elections from 1932-1944. In fact, Roosevelt was reelected in 1936 by an even larger and even more historic margin than he had in 1932. In 1936, President Roosevelt carried every state in the Union except Vermont and Maine, winning 523 electoral votes to his opponent's 8. Roosevelt carried more than 60% of the popular vote, the most of any President in history at the time.

The 1940 Republican National Convention was televised, though there were almost no television sets in the nation at the time. It was broadcast on the fledgling NBC stations in New York City, Philadelphia and Albany, New York. What made bigger headlines, however, was the announcement weeks later that two bombs had been found at the site where the convention had been held. The *Associated Press* reported, "Two powerful dynamite bombs were found near the convention hall during the republican national convention in Philadelphia two weeks ago, it was learned from a high police authority today after Police Commissioner Lewis J. Valentine disclosed a number of bombs were found during the meeting. Valentine did not say how many bombs were found nor where they were discovered, but other sources said seven or eight were located, some of them in a hall frequently used for communist meetings. Valentine made the disclosure in a talk to his detective force in which he. asserted that the bomb explosion at the world's fair July 4 which killed two detectives 'is just the beginning.' Lieut. James Fyke (head of the bomb and forgery squad), went to Philadelphia while the republican convention was in session," Valentine said. 'Some bombs were found there, and he opened two of them.'"

Though the disclosure elicited some national sympathy, this by no means translated into votes, and America would survive the Great Depression, World War II and a war with Korea before a Republican would be in office again. On January 20th, 1941, Roosevelt became the first President to be inaugurated for a third term, and much like his first swearing-in, his third inauguration came amidst a major crisis. War was ravaging Europe, with Nazi Germany conquering much of the continent. In response, the U.S. gradually shifted from its neutral stance. In March, Roosevelt signed the Lend-Lease Act, which authorized the President to give arms to any nation if it was in US national interest. With this act, the US was able to support Great Britain without declaring war on Nazi Germany or Italy.

Given that Roosevelt won a smashing victory in 1940, the 1940 Republican National Convention has been mentioned an unusual amount of times in 2016 due to the similarities between Donald Trump and the eventual Republican nominee in 1940, Wendell Willkie. This is because both men were businessmen with limited political experience who were distrusted by vast swathes of the party for having views considered antithetical to previous Republican platforms. In Willkie's case, he changed parties the year before the 1940 election.

Another reason Willkie's name has been bandied about is because he didn't actually run for the presidency during the primaries, which still did not have any influence over the choice of delegates. He was chosen at a deadlocked, brokered convention, a possibility that hovered over the 2016 Republican primaries for much of the process.

Willkie

Chapter 8: Resurgence

"Speaking in a very personal sense, I express my deep gratitude to this convention for the tribute you have paid to the best campaigner in the Nixon family-my wife Pat. In honoring her, you have honored millions of women in America who have contributed in the past and will contribute in the future so very much to better government in this country. Again, as I did last night when I was not at the convention, I express the appreciation of all of the delegates and of all America for letting us see young America at its best at our convention. As I express my appreciation to you, I want to say that you have inspired us with your enthusiasm, with your intelligence, with your dedication at this convention. You have made us realize that this is a year when we can prove the experts' predictions wrong, because we can set as our goal winning a majority of the new voters for our ticket this November. I pledge to you, all of the new voters in America who are listening on television and listening here in this convention hall, that I will do everything that I can over these next 4 years to make your support be one that you can be proud of, because as I said to you last night, and I feel it very deeply in my heart: Years from now I want you to look back and be able to say that your first vote was one of the best votes you ever cast in your life." - Richard Nixon, accepting his party's nomination to the Presidency at the 1972 Republican National Convention

When the Republican Party met in National Convention in 1952, it had every reason to feel optimistic. The Democratic incumbent, Harry S Truman, had announced he would not seek to be elected for a second full term (having served since 1945 after Roosevelt's death). Therefore, the field was wide open for the party to take back the White House.

Although it seems impossible to believe now, many widely assumed that Dwight D. Eisenhower would never be president after he failed to enter politics in 1948. That year, President Truman tried to convince Eisenhower to be his Vice-Presidential candidate, aware that his unpopularity would be boosted by a war hero every American admired. At the same time, making Eisenhower his Vice President would clear Ike's path to the presidency in 1952. When Eisenhower refused the offer, it was widely assumed that Truman would lose to Dewey, who would then presumably be positioned to be president until 1956, at which point Ike would be 66 years old, too old to be president.

Eisenhower

As it turned out, Truman famously won reelection in 1948 by the slimmest of margins over

Dewey, meaning the path was clear for Eisenhower to run in 1952 if he so chose. Eisenhower mulled over the decision to run for President for months, even while a Draft Eisenhower Movement had sprung up in an eager effort to encourage his run. Having failed to get Eisenhower to be his Vice President, Truman now suggested Eisenhower should replace him, as a Democrat.

There was one question that remained unresolved: was Eisenhower a Democrat or a Republican? For many, including Truman, the answer was of little importance, and for Eisenhower himself the answer seemed insignificant. But the General needed to decided one way or the other before he could expect to run a successful campaign. Previously, Eisenhower was not much of a partisan or an ideologue. Because of the dominance of the Democratic Party since the beginning of the Great Depression, many suspected he would play it safe and run with the party of Jefferson and Jackson.

Instead, however, Eisenhower chose the Party of Lincoln. Despite Truman's insistence that he run as a Democrat, Eisenhower thought the party favored too much centralization in government, and he preferred the ideology of the Republican Party. Still, even after choosing a party, Eisenhower had still not decided to run. Previously, there were two separate Draft Eisenhower Movements: one in each party. With his announcement of Republican allegiance, the Democratic Draft Movement died. The Republican one, however, gained steam.

Hoping to convince Eisenhower to run, New York Governor Thomas Dewey and Massachusetts Senator Henry Cabot Lodge entered Eisenhower's name into the upcoming New Hampshire Primary without the "candidate's" knowledge. The two were especially eager to nominate Eisenhower, fearing that the ultra conservative Senator Taft of Ohio would win the nomination and sink the party's prospects for decades.

On the night of the primary, Eisenhower won by a landslide. With that, he captured all of the state's delegates, and he also had enormous momentum to carry towards the nomination. The next day, he finally relented and announced that New Hampshire voters had flattered him, and he would be honored to run for President.

With that, Eisenhower quickly won the Republican nomination, and while speaking to the convention gathered in Chicago, Ike hit all the right notes with post-World War II Republicans, saying, "Ladies and Gentlemen, you have summoned me on behalf of millions of your fellow Americans to lead a great crusade—for Freedom in America and Freedom in the world. I know something of the solemn responsibility of leading a crusade. I have led one. I take up this task, therefore, in a spirit of deep obligation. Mindful of its burdens and of its decisive importance. I accept your summons. I will lead this crusade. Our aims—the aims of this Republican crusade—are clear: to sweep from office an administration which has fastened on every one of us the wastefulness, the arrogance and corruption in high places, the heavy bur-dens and anxieties which are the bitter fruit of a party too long in power. Much more than this, it is our aim to give to our country a program of progressive policies drawn from our finest Republican traditions; to unite us wherever we have been divided; to strengthen freedom wherever among any group is has been weakened; to build a sure foundation for sound prosperity for all here at home and for a just and sure peace throughout our world. ... Before this I stood on the eve of battle. Before every attack it has always been my practice to seek out our men in their camps and on the roads and talk with them face to face about their concerns and discuss with them the great mission to which we were all committed. In this battle to which all of us are now committed it will be my practice to meet and talk with Americans face to face in every section, every corner, every nook and cranny of this land."

A picture of the 1952 Republican convention

Eisenhower was nominated at a time when Truman's Democratic administration was historically unpopular as a result of the Korean War. Given Eisenhower's reputation and the Democrats' unpopularity, 1952 was shaping up to be a landslide. In fact, the Eisenhower ticket's biggest problem was the Vice Presidential candidate, California Senator Richard Nixon, who it was alleged had improperly received funds from a secret trust. on September 23, 1952, Nixon allayed fears of corruption with his infamous "Checkers Speech", and it would be another 20 years before the American public discovered that Nixon was indeed a crook. Nevertheless, the damage Nixon caused created terse relations between Ike and his Vice President, which would come back to haunt Nixon in the Election of 1960.

The candidates for the 1960 election were not on firm footing with the changing format of presidential politics. The advent of television was strange to both men, and the more transparent nomination system that came into effect some years later did not function in the same way as it does in modern times. This included the use of primaries to test the waters and to practice one's presentation to the public in preparation for later and larger events. The actual decisions were often made by fewer people, and in relative secrecy, in the infamous smoke-filled rooms where party bosses negotiated out of the public eye.

While Kennedy had to field numerous challenges from within his party, and issues of his religion from mainly Protestant America, Nixon was largely unencumbered on the right except for a possible challenge mounted by Nelson Rockefeller. Nixon, however, made some mistakes up front, such as promising to campaign in every state, which required him to spend valuable time in states he could not win, or states with few electoral votes. During the campaign, he would be forced into a two-week hospital stay due to an injury, and despite using his own advertisements as camera practice for the coming debates, he was singularly uninformed of the subtleties required by the medium, despite his rhetorical abilities.

Also potentially working against Nixon was his inability to distinguish himself from Kennedy in the stark ways he had against previous opponents. The wide chasm of modern liberal and conservative stances is far different than the divide in the 1960s; Nixon, by today's standards, would not be deemed a true conservative, and JFK was far less liberal than the modern voter might think, as he is often mistakenly lumped in ideologically with his brother Ted. Both were pro-civil rights, but JFK's intervention on behalf of Martin Luther King gave him a decided edge. Both were against the FDR New Deal and the welfare system in general. One of their only differences may have been a general tendency on the part of Nixon toward "hawkishness." A common difficulty for both parties was that Nixon and Kennedy were strongly disliked in the south due to their support of the civil rights movement.

Nixon chose as his vice president Henry Cabot Lodge from Massachusetts, in a sense invading Kennedy's strongest territory. And while Nixon did not make a major case of Kennedy's religion, many Protestant ministers did. The only previous Catholic candidate had been Al Smith, who was defeated soundly by the only other Quaker president, Herbert Hoover. Groups for religious freedom contended that Kennedy's Catholicism would make governing the nation as President difficult. Many were suspicious that he would accept demands from the Pope and the Catholic Hierarchy, but by September, Kennedy closed the issue in a speech in Houston, where he said he was running to be a "President who happens to be Catholic," not a "Catholic President." For the remainder of the campaign, Kennedy's religion no longer fascinated the media, though it was likely still privately on the minds of many voters.

Passing on the religious question, "the Republicans portrayed Nixon as the son of a hard-working middle class family and highly experienced world statesman. They portrayed Kennedy as a rich little boy who was more interested in chasing women than meeting his obligations..."[2] Kennedy, on the other hand, viewed Nixon as a "hothead," but he was less successful in making the label stick to his opponent. In selling himself, however, Kennedy did well, and made much of his war record of decorated heroic actions. Nixon countered with his anti-communism credentials, attempting to once more ride the wave of public sentiment against infiltration of public and private institutions by red operatives, but Kennedy couldn't be painted soft on communism either.

In the election of 1960, Eisenhower publicly supported his Vice President in his bid for the White House. In private, however, Eisenhower had reservations about Nixon, and was not terribly displeased when he lost to Kennedy. Kennedy himself, despite being a Democrat, had supported Eisenhower over Stevenson in '52 and '56. As it turned out, Eisenhower may have harmed Nixon's chances when he publicly campaigned for Nixon in the waning days of the election that Fall. After giving a press conference, reporters asked Eisenhower to name a policy idea proposed by Nixon that he had adopted, to which Eisenhower responded, "If you give me a week, I might think of one. I don't remember." Though Eisenhower intended it as a joke, Kennedy's campaign seized upon the gaffe, using it as a quote in its own campaign commercials. Kennedy, of course, would go on to win that fall in one of the closest elections in American history.

On Election Day, the popular vote was as close as polls suggested: Kennedy won by a hair, with 49.7% to Nixon's 49.5%. The Electoral College vote, however, was a different story, with Kennedy winning with 303 votes to Nixon's 219. In Mississippi, eight unpledged delegates went to Strom Thurmond and Harry Byrd, one to Byrd and one to Goldwater in Oklahoma, and six for Byrd in Alabama.

In the wake of the Kennedy assassination, many Republicans sensed an opening, but the 1964 convention became controversial for choosing an insurgent conservative candidate: Senator Barry Goldwater of Arizona. The party broke history by disregarding its moderate wing and nominating Barry Goldwater, assisted in part by what was considered Nelson Rockfeller's scandalous relationship with his second wife.

---

[2] American Political Buttons; Election of 1960 - americanpoliticalbuttons.com

Goldwater

Goldwater assured the gathered convention, "From this moment, united and determined, we will go forward together, dedicated to the ultimate and undeniable greatness of the whole man. Together we will win. I accept your nomination with a deep sense of humility. I accept, too, the responsibility that goes with it, and I seek your continued help and your continued guidance. My fellow Republicans, our cause is too great for any man to feel worthy of it. Our task would be too great for any man, did he not have with him the heart and the hands of this great Republican Party, and I promise you tonight that every fiber of my being is consecrated to our cause; that nothing shall be lacking from the struggle that can be brought to it by enthusiasm, by devotion, and plain hard work. In this world no person, no party can guarantee anything, but what we can do and what we shall do is to deserve victory, and victory will be ours. The good Lord raised this mighty Republic to be a home for the brave and to flourish as the land of the free-not to stagnate in the swampland of collectivism, not to cringe before the bully of communism. Now, my fellow Americans, the tide has been running against freedom. Our people have followed false prophets. We must, and we shall, return to proven ways-- not because they are old, but because they are true. We must, and we shall, set the tide running again in the cause of freedom. And this party, with its every action, every word, every breath, and every heartbeat, has but a single resolve, and that is freedom - freedom made orderly for this nation by our constitutional government; freedom under a government limited by laws of nature and of nature's God; freedom - balanced so that liberty lacking order will not become the slavery of the prison cell; balanced so that liberty lacking order will not become the license of the mob and of the jungle."

Goldwater has long been considered one of modern presidential history's most conservative candidates, and he wasn't afraid to promote politically unpopular views. During Eisenhower's presidency, Goldwater had advocated a hard-line against communism and criticized Ike for not balancing the budget. At the time, Goldwater was running against the grain of his own party; the Republican Party's political tactics since the New Deal had involved accommodating the New Deal legislation while aiming to limit any additional government programs. The moderates in the Republican Party never promised to roll back any of the programs that were already in place, which included very popular programs like Social Security and the FDIC. Goldwater, however, scrapped that Republican pledge and vowed to undo much of the New Deal.

His political goals proved toxic. Pledging to make social security voluntary made many Americans remember American policy before the Great Depression. On civil rights, Goldwater hoped to win the segregationist South by vowing to disband all civil rights legislation, but in so doing he alienated the party's Northern base. Johnson, meanwhile, was himself a Southerner who was now ready to claim much of the North. This left Goldwater with little base to rest his ambitions upon.

Goldwater also took strong stances on foreign policy, allowing Johnson to paint him as an extremist. For example, Goldwater suggested that military field officers ought to be allowed to use nuclear weapons in Vietnam, which led the Johnson campaign to run the most controversial political ad in American history. In the famous "Daisy" ad, a little girl starts counting while pulling petals off a flower, and as she starts counting down, an ominous voice begins a countdown followed by a nuclear explosion. The notorious ad implied that Goldwater's policies risked the destruction of the world, and thus a vote for Goldwater could lead to nuclear war. A similar ad would be used in 1984 by presidential candidate Walter Mondale against Ronald Reagan himself.

The Daisy Ad is the most famous part of the 1964 landslide. On Election Day, Johnson won one of the largest popular vote tallies in history, with over 61% of the votes cast. In the Electoral College, he also won big, with all but five Southern states and Goldwater's Arizona. As he expected, the South was lost, but his victories elsewhere were large and solid enough to allow Johnson to easily secure election to the White House.

In 1968, when the party met in Miami Beach, the Republicans were ready to present themselves to America as the solution to the country's deepening woes. Johnson was so unpopular thanks to Vietnam that he refused to run again, and when Bobby Kennedy was assassinated and riots marred the Democratic convention in Chicago, it seemed the Republicans were in good shape.

At the convention, the party went out of its way to portray itself as understanding the problems of the nation: "Tens of thousands of young men have died or been wounded in Vietnam. Many young people are losing faith in our society. Our inner cities have become centers of despair. Millions of Americans are caught in the cycle of poverty—poor education, unemployment or serious under-employment, and the inability to afford decent housing. Inflation has eroded confidence in the dollar at home and abroad. It has severely cut into the incomes of all families, the jobless, the farmers, the retired and those living on fixed incomes and pensions. Today's Americans are uncertain about the future, and frustrated about the recent past. America urgently needs new leadership—leadership courageous and understanding—leadership that will recapture control of events, mastering them rather than permitting them to master us, thus restoring our confidence in ourselves and in our future. Our need is new leadership which will develop imaginative new approaches assuring full opportunity to all our citizens—leadership which will face and resolve the basic problems of our country. Our Convention in 1968 can spark a 'Republican Resurgence' under men and women willing to face the realities of the world in which we live."

The man they chose was a familiar face. How Richard Nixon accomplished such a complete resurrection as a central figure of national politics is still viewed as a historical wonder, especially following two such bitter defeats at the national and state level (when he lost the race for governor of California). However, the drive to stay relevant within his party, and an uncanny gift for reinventing himself, brought Nixon back from the political dead. By 1967, he was declaring his intentions to run for the presidency again, despite his wife Pat's misgivings.

For the election of 1968, several circumstances tended toward a Nixon advantage. First, the available challengers in the Republican Party were, for one reason or another, not suited to serve as party frontrunners. George Romney enjoyed a brief time as an anti-war candidate, but that constituency could not sustain him on the national stage, and his comment about being "brainwashed" on Vietnam did him in politically. Barry Goldwater had already been hopelessly defeated by President Johnson in 1964, and the "new conservative star,"[3] Ronald Reagan, had never yet held public office. Reagan was obligated to try his hand at the state level by first running for the governorship of California. Liberals of the party generally lined up behind Nelson Rockefeller, but they were not a strong faction that year, especially with the troubles facing the Democrats.

Nixon had not really made his move yet, but he was immediately aided in his vault to the front by Lyndon Johnson's comment that Nixon was a "chronic campaigner."[4] In a way that the Democrats could not hope to demonstrate in 1968, the Republican Convention was a display of congeniality and unity, despite the various factions supporting a separate candidate each. Choosing Marylander Spiro Agnew as his running mate, Nixon won the nomination on the first ballot, with Reagan moving to make it unanimous. Conservatives such as Goldwater and Thurmond immediately joined in the support. From that moment, the results of Nixon's work

---

[3] Miller Center - *Richard M. Nixon* - www.millercenter.org.
[4] Miller Center

since the 1962 defeat took effect, and he demonstrated himself to be a far more thoughtful and careful candidate than in the past. The image of a "New Nixon" emerged, "more statesmanlike, less combative , more mature and presidential."[5]

In accepting his party's nomination, Nixon told those gathered, "The time has come for honest government in the United States of America. And so tonight I do not promise the millennium in the morning. I don't promise that we can eradicate poverty, and end discrimination, eliminate all danger of war in the space of four, or even eight years. But, I do promise action -- a new policy for peace abroad; a new policy for peace and progress and justice at home. Look at our problems abroad. Do you realize that we face the stark truth that we are worse off in every area of the world tonight than we were when President Eisenhower left office eight years ago. That's the record. And there is only one answer to such a record of failure and that is a complete housecleaning of those responsible for the failures of that record. The answer is a complete re-appraisal of America's policies in every section of the world. We shall begin with Vietnam. We all hope in this room that there is a chance that current negotiations may bring an honorable end to that war. And we will say nothing during this campaign that might destroy that chance."

He refused to debate the Democratic candidate at all, rather than walk into any sort of ambush as he had in 1960, and given that he enjoyed a double-digit lead at the time, he saw no reason to risk it. Hubert Humphrey had won the Democratic nomination in one of the ugliest convention displays in the annals of American history, choosing Maine's Edmund Muskie as his running mate. Police intervention on the convention floor and the subsequent large-scale violence experienced on live television from Chicago left the Democratic Party shattered and running from far behind. In an additional twist, Alabaman George Wallace mounted a national campaign as the candidate for the American Independent Party, receiving significant support in the Deep South.

Through all of this, Nixon remained steady, ensuring he was portrayed "as a figure of stability in a time of national upheaval. Nixon promised a return to traditional values and 'law and order.'"[6] Nixon's alleged "Southern strategy," which challenged Democratic liberals to more openly defend their liberal positions, was intended to capture the entire south for the Republican Party in a lasting voting bloc, which if true, was a successful gambit on Nixon's part. Some refute the notion of such a strategy, however, or at least of its abiding success, reminding us that "the growth of GOP support among white southerners was mostly steady and mostly gradual from 1928 to 2010."[7] Perhaps most notoriously, Nixon scuttled peace talks to end the Vietnam War until after he was elected.

In winning the 1968 election by a popular margin of almost half a million votes (but in an

[5] Miller Center

[6] Nixon Presidential Library & Museum

[7] Dan McLaughlin, *The Southern Strategy Myth and the Lost Majority: How Republicans Really Lost the South,* Red State, Jan. 11, 2014

electoral landslide), Nixon had abandoned the one-trick strategy of anti-communism and replaced it with a plan to withdraw from Vietnam without the country appearing to be weak, promises to restore law and order to a society in chaos, and to represent what he termed the "great silent majority."[8]

Chapter 9: A Party United, With Positive Programs

"I am very proud of our party tonight. This convention has shown to all America a party united, with positive programs for solving the nation's problems; a party ready to build a new consensus with all those across the land who share a community of values embodied in these words: family, work, neighborhood, peace and freedom. I know we have had a quarrel or two, but only as to the method of attaining a goal. There was no argument about the goal. ... More than anything else, I want my candidacy to unify our country; to renew the American spirit and sense of purpose. I want to carry our message to every American, regardless of party affiliation, who is a member of this community of shared values. ... The major issue of this campaign is the direct political, personal and moral responsibility of Democratic Party leadership--in the White House and in Congress--for this unprecedented calamity which has befallen us. They tell us they have done the most that humanly could be done. They say that the United States has had its day in the sun; that our nation has passed its zenith. ... My fellow citizens, I utterly reject that view. The American people, the most generous on earth, who created the highest standard of living, are not going to accept the notion that we can only make a better world for others by moving backwards ourselves. Those who believe we can have no business leading the nation." - Ronald Reagan, accepting the Republican National Convention's nomination in 1980

Nixon had scored a solid win for his party when he ran in 1968, and four years later, Pat Nixon, his wife, became the first First Lady to speak at a Republican National Convention, praising her husband and telling the American people, "I stay in the wings and don't come out in front too often, so this is quite unusual for me, but I do want to thank all of you for your friendship and your loyal support and for planning this wonderful evening for me. I shall remember it always. And thanks to the young people for this great welcome."

---

[8] Nixon Presidential Library & Museum

Pat Nixon speaking at the 1972 Republican National Convention

Her husband won re-election easily, but by then Watergate was already starting to become an issue. The president became embroiled in the cover-up of a break-in by men affiliated with his re-election campaign into the headquarters of the Democratic National Convention at the Watergate office complex in 1972. Eventually Nixon's role in this and other illegal campaign activities became known, and in 1974 he resigned from office in disgrace rather than face impeachment. Gerald Ford, Nixon's vice president, assumed the presidency.

Not surprisingly, Nixon's behavior tainted the entire party and sent it into disarray. Ford, a decent man but uninspiring leader, ran for the nomination in 1976, but the problems of Nixon and the country at the time led to the rise of a rare situation in American politics: a time when an incumbent was challenged for the nomination. In 1976, Ronald Reagan, the former Governor of California, got enough delegates to make him a contender for his party's nomination. Reagan ran a hard and aggressive campaign against Ford, who had blotted his record by pardoning Richard Nixon.

Ultimately, enough party leaders were loyal, and in the end Ford received the mixed blessing that was the Republican nomination at that time. He told the convention, "I have been called an unelected President, an accidental President. We may even hear that again from the other party, despite the fact that I was welcomed and endorsed by an overwhelming majority of their elected representatives in the Congress who certified my fitness to our highest office. Having become

Vice President and President without expecting or seeking either, I have a special feeling toward these high offices. To me, the Presidency and the Vice-Presidency were not prizes to be won, but a duty to be done. ... Two years ago, on August 9, 1974, I placed my hand on the Bible, which Betty held, and took the same constitutional oath that was administered to George Washington. I had faith in our people, in our institutions, and in myself. 'My fellow Americans,' I said, 'our long national nightmare is over.' It was an hour in our history that troubled our minds and tore at our hearts. Anger and hatred had risen to dangerous levels, dividing friends and families. The polarization of our political order had aroused unworthy passions of reprisal and revenge. Our governmental system was closer to stalemate than at any time since Abraham Lincoln took the same oath of office. Our economy was in the throes of runaway inflation, taking us headlong into the worst recession since Franklin D. Roosevelt took the same oath. On that dark day I told my fellow countrymen, 'I am acutely aware that you have not elected me as your President by your ballots, so I ask you to confirm me as your President with your prayers.'"

As it turned out, Ford remained an unelected president, losing the 1976 campaign Democrat Jimmy Carter, and for the Republican Party, and the country at large, things would have to get much worse before that got any better.

By the time the Republicans met again in 1980, the country was ready for change, and Republicans believed that Ronald Reagan was the man who could give it to them. He was nominated quickly and went on to win the election handily, bringing hope back to the country from the very moment he said, during his inauguration, "We have every right to dream heroic dreams. Those who say that we're in a time when there are not heroes, they just don't know where to look. You can see heroes every day going in and out of factory gates. Others, a handful in number, produce enough food to feed all of us and then the world beyond. You meet heroes across a counter, and they're on both sides of that counter. There are entrepreneurs with faith in themselves and faith in an idea who create new jobs, new wealth and opportunity. They're individuals and families whose taxes support the government and whose voluntary gifts support church, charity, culture, art, and education. Their patriotism is quiet, but deep. Their values sustain our national life. Now, I have used the words 'they' and 'their' in speaking of these heroes. I could say 'you' and 'your,' because I'm addressing the heroes of whom I speak—you, the citizens of this blessed land. Your dreams, your hopes, your goals are going to be the dreams, the hopes, and the goals of this administration, so help me God. We shall reflect the compassion that is so much a part of your makeup. How can we love our country and not love our countrymen; and loving them, reach out a hand when they fall, heal them when they're sick, and provide opportunity to make them self-sufficient so they will be equal in fact and not just in theory? Can we solve the problems confronting us? Well, the answer is an unequivocal and emphatic 'yes.' To paraphrase Winston Churchill, I did not take the oath I've just taken with the intention of presiding over the dissolution of the world's strongest economy."

Reagan and his wife at the 1980 Republican convention

Reagan's words reinvigorated the party and the nation, leading to one of the most enthusiastic conventions in the party's history in 1984. The Republican National Convention chose Reagan and his Vice President, George H.W. Bush, to run for yet another term. The two men were elected in a landslide and the party had no problem choosing his successor. In 1988, Bush accepted his party's nomination to the presidency, vowing to continue the programs Reagan had put in place: "For seven and a half years I have helped a President conduct the most difficult job on earth. Ronald Reagan asked for, and received, my candor. He never asked for, but he did receive, my loyalty. Those of you who saw the President's speech this week, and listened to the simple truth of his words, will understand my loyalty all these years. But now you must see me for what I am: The Republican candidate for President of the United States. And now I turn to the American people to share my hopes and intentions, and why - and where - I wish to lead.

And so tonight is for big things. But I'll try to be fair to the other side. I'll try to hold my charisma in check. I reject the temptation to engage in personal references. My approach this evening is, as Sergeant Joe Friday used to say, "Just the facts, ma'am." After all, the facts are on our side. I seek the presidency for a single purpose, a purpose that has motivated millions of Americans across the years and the ocean voyages. I seek the presidency to build a better America. It is that simple - and that big. I am a man who sees life in terms of missions - missions defined and missions completed. When I was a torpedo bomber pilot they defined the mission for us. Before we took off we all understood that no matter what, you try to reach the target. There have been other missions for me - Congress, China, the CIA. But I am here tonight - and I am your candidate - because the most important work of my life is to complete the mission we started in 1980. How do we complete it? We build it."

Bush won in 1988, but by the end of his four year term, the party was again in disarray, as factions sprung up that differed on how best to carry out the party's goals. Pat Buchanan, who had challenged the Bush for the nomination, later threw support behind the president and coined a new phrase when he gave a speech at the 1992 convention: "Friends, this election is about more than who gets what. It is about who we are. It is about what we believe and what we stand for as Americans. There is a religious war going on in this country. It is a cultural war, as critical to the kind of nation we shall be as the Cold War itself. For this war is for the soul of America. And in that struggle for the soul of America, Clinton & Clinton are on the other side, and George Bush is on our side. And so to the Buchanan Brigades out there, we have to come home and stand beside George Bush."

Since that time, the term "culture wars" has been a popular phrase among conservatives concerned about declining American morals. George Bush lost the 1992 election, and some blamed Buchanan's strident words, but Bush was vindicated on a certain level when, eight years later, the party met again to nominate another Bush, his son and namesake, making the Republican Party the first in American history to nominate the son of a previous president for the nation's highest office (John Adams and his son, John Quincy, were nominated by two different parties.).

In accepting the party's nomination in 2000, George W. Bush told those present, "I want to thank my father -- the most decent man I have ever known. All my life I have been amazed that a gentle soul could be so strong. And Dad, I want you to know how proud I am to be your son. My father was the last president of a great generation. A generation of Americans who stormed beaches, liberated concentration camps and delivered us from evil. ... Now the question comes to the sons and daughters of this achievement.... This is a remarkable moment in the life of our nation. Never has the promise of prosperity been so vivid. But times of plenty, like times of crisis, are tests of American character. Prosperity can be a tool in our hands -- used to build and better our country. Or it can be a drug in our system -- dulling our sense of urgency, of empathy, of duty. Our opportunities are too great, our lives too short, to waste this moment. So tonight we vow to our nation ... We will seize this moment of American promise. We will use these good times for great goals. We will confront the hard issues -- threats to our national security, threats to our health and retirement security -- before the challenges of our time become crises for our children. And we will extend the promise of prosperity to every forgotten corner of this country. To every man and woman, a chance to succeed. To every child, a chance to learn. To every family, a chance to live with dignity and hope. Those who did put their medals in drawers, went to work, and built on a heroic scale ... highways and universities, suburbs and factories, great cities and grand alliances -- the strong foundations of an American Century."

Bush won his 2000 election and returned to the White House in 2004 after he accepted his party's nomination during a convention held in New York City with these words: "Thank you all. Mr. Chairman, delegates, fellow citizens: I am honored by your support, and I accept your nomination for President of the United States. When I said those words 4 years ago, none of us could have envisioned what these years would bring. In the heart of this great city, we saw tragedy arrive on a quiet morning. We saw the bravery of rescuers grow with danger. We learned of passengers on a doomed plane who died with a courage that frightened their killers. We have seen a shaken economy rise to its feet. And we have seen Americans in uniform storming mountain strongholds and charging through sandstorms and liberating millions with acts of valor that would make the men of Normandy proud. Since 2001, Americans have been given hills to climb and found the strength to climb them. Now, because we have made the hard journey, we can see the valley below. Now, because we have faced challenges with resolve, we have historic goals within our reach and greatness in our future. We will build a safer world and a more hopeful America, and nothing will hold us back."

To date, Bush remains the last Republican to serve as president. The candidates chosen to run in 2008 and 2012 lost their runs to Barack Obama, the first African-American president. Though Obama is a Democrat, those who know history remember that he might not have ever risen to such an office had the founders of the Republican Party not met over 150 years earlier to oppose the extension of slavery across the country. Given that fact, and the unsettled nature of the Republican Party in the wake of the 2016 primaries, it is a telling reminder that even amidst all the partisanship of the 21st century, the strength of the American electoral system has always ensured that no matter what disagreements may develop, all members of both parties remain bound together by a shared history.

Online Resources

<u>Other books about American history</u> by Charles River Editors

<u>Other books about the Republican Party</u> on Amazon

Bibliography

Greeley, Horace. *Proceedings of the first three Republican national conventions of 1856, 1860 and 1864* (2012)

Library of Congress. Republican National Political Conventions: 1856-2008 (2011)

Milton, Raleigh. *Thirty-First Republican National Convention Kansas City 1976* (1976)

Tweedy, John. *A History of the Republican National Conventions from 1856 to 1908* (1910)

Yob, John P. Chaos. *The Outsider's Guide to a Contested Republican National Convention* (2016)

37991648R00044

Printed in Great Britain
by Amazon